The Pastor as Teacher

PASTORAL MINISTRY SERIES

The Pastor as Teacher

EDITED BY

Earl E. Shelp
and
Ronald H. Sunderland

The Pilgrim Press
NEW YORK

Library of Congress Cataloging-in-Publication Data

The Pastor as teacher / edited by Earl E. Shelp and Ronald H.
  Sunderland.
      p.   cm. — (Pastoral ministry series)
  "Originally presented during the spring of 1987 as the Parker memorial lectures in theology and ministry at the Institute of Religion in Houston. Texas"—P. vii.
      Contents: Holy place, teaching place / Maria Harris—Teaching as witness / Walter Brueggemann — Transmitting the Jewish heritage from generation to generation / Samuel E. Karff — The teaching function of liturgy / Stanley Samuel Harakas — A moral magisterium in ecumenical perspective / Richard A. McCormick — Religious teaching in secular form / James M. Wall.
      ISBN 0-8298-0812-4
      1. Clergy—Office. 2. Rabbis—Office. 3. Teaching—Religious aspects—Christianity. 4. Teaching—Religious aspects—Judaism.
  I. Shelp,, Earl E., 1947–   . II. Sunderland, Ronald, 1929–
  III. Title: Parker memorial lectures in theology and ministry.
  IV. Series.
  BV660.2.P2645   1989
  268—dc20   89-35065

The Pilgrim Press, 475 Riverside Dr., New York, NY 10115

Contents

Contributors

WALTER BRUEGGEMANN is professor of Old Testament, Columbia Theological Seminary, Decatur, Georgia.

STANLEY SAMUEL HARAKAS is Archbishop Iakovos Professor of Orthodox Theology, Holy Cross Greek Orthodox School of Theology, Brookline, Massachusetts.

MARIA HARRIS is visiting professor of religious education, Fordham University, and professor of religious education, New York University.

SAMUEL E. KARFF is rabbi at Congregation Beth Israel, Houston, Texas.

RICHARD A. McCORMICK, S.J., is John A. O'Brien Professor of Christian Ethics, Department of Theology, University of Notre Dame, Notre Dame, Indiana.

EARL E. SHELP is executive director and senior fellow, Foundation for Interfaith Research and Ministry, Houston, Texas.

RONALD H. SUNDERLAND is associate director and research fellow, Foundation for Interfaith Research and Ministry, Houston, Texas.

JAMES M. WALL is editor of the *Christian Century*, Chicago, Illinois.

Acknowledgments

THESE ESSAYS WERE ORIGINALLY PRESENTED DURING THE
spring of 1987 as the Parker Memorial Lectures in Theology
and Ministry at the Institute of Religion in Houston, Texas.
Funding for this fourth annual series of lectures was provided
in loving memory of R. A. Parker by a donor who wished to
remain anonymous. Mr. Parker was a committed and tireless
trustee of the Institute of Religion. His contribution to the life
of the institute and to the ministry of the church is perpetu-
ated through the publication of this volume and the preceding
volumes in this Pastoral Ministry Series. The generosity of the
individual who underwrote the lectures is gratefully acknowledged.

Appreciation is also expressed to J. Robert Nelson, director
of the Institute of Religion, for his support of this project.
Trustees of the institute are thanked for their interest and
commitment to this aspect of the institute's educational and
outreach program. The authors personally presented their
ideas and insights in lecture form to audiences at the Institute
of Religion. The extension of their work in published form
through this volume constitutes a second reason to express
appreciation to them.

Finally, appreciation is expressed to those individuals who
assisted in preparing the final manuscripts for publication. Ed
DuBose, research assistant to the editors, Juanita Veasey,
secretary to Earl Shelp, and Marion M. Meyer, editor at the
Pilgrim Press, each had an important role in shepherding the
transformation of the text from manuscript to book form. To all
of these individuals the editors express their gratitude.

Introduction

Earl E. Shelp and Ronald H. Sunderland

THE ORGANIZATION OF CONGREGATIONAL LEADERSHIP AND life seems increasingly to resemble corporate or business structures. It is not uncommon to find in large or even medium-size congregations professional staffing patterns, policies, and procedures that would warm the heart of most management professors. Specialized ministries and ministers are often viewed as indications of a congregation's sophistication, size, diversity, and commitment to programs of high quality. Thus, churches have pastors or senior ministers, associate and assistant pastors, each with a unique job description, and ministers of music, pastoral care, recreation, social work, and education for every age-group—children, youth, single adults, adults, and senior adults. Whether justified on biblical, theological, managerial, economic, or utilitarian grounds, a trend toward a segregation of roles and specialization of ministries seems firmly in place. Proficiency and productivity, virtues borrowed perhaps from secular life, have become desired attributes and criteria for evaluation within many congregations.

We make no judgments about the value of vocational specialization or the segregation of roles and functions in church life. Rather, we call attention to the phenomenon in order to highlight the demarcation of responsibilities and accountability within contemporary churches. In a situation where the defining features of community and identity are disjointed,

1

what is the risk that the identity and life of the community may be so fragmented that the integrity of the community and faith will be weakened or lost? Or, can there be points or programs, in such a situation, where the separate pieces of community and identity are brought together for one and all to form a cohesive and coherent whole? If teaching is an important means by which faith, broadly understood, can be interpreted, understood, professed, and lived, then when, where, how, and by whom should it occur?

In an age of specialization, teaching tends to be an activity relegated to the church school, and learning is the desired result. Pastors appear content to delegate instructional tasks to others so that precious scarce time may be invested in the preparation of sermons and the design of worship. Yet, as the contributors to this volume argue, teaching is not the sort of religious duty that can be assigned to others easily or ignored with impunity. Rather, teaching what is believed about God and God's will for human life is an individual and communal responsibility. How these responsibilities may be understood and why they ought to be met by pastors, laypeople, congregations, denominations, and even secular media are related questions to which the contributors offer insightful, provocative, and challenging answers.

Maria Harris begins the discussion of the task of teaching with a consideration of the sanctuary as a setting for education. She acknowledges that sanctuaries primarily are places for worship, proclamation, and interpretation. Nevertheless, she argues that the whole community, past and present, is the primary agent of Christian education and that the pastor, as representative of the body of Christ, has an instructional role. The pastor presides at worship and leads in prayer, both of which, according to Harris, are educative. The pastor is therefore an educator, and Harris develops her understanding of a pastor's educational role in worship through discussions of the sanctuary as a place of mystery, listening, questioning, artistry, and resurrection. Properly understood and acted upon, the sanctuary, she claims, is and ought to be a place for education where profound lessons about human life and God can be learned.

Walter Brueggemann shares Harris's concerns for the communal character of religious instruction, which he finds rooted in the witness of Moses. Through an enlightening survey of Jewish scripture, Brueggemann argues that teaching in the Old Testament "urges a particular perspective on reality" and "mediates to the learner a distinct identity and vocation." It aims at the creation of a distinctive community and constitutes a witness to a "particular truth claim, to the exclusion of other truth claims."

The witness of Moses and his successors that Israel was to be an alternative community embracing Yahweh and accepting a specific destiny and vocation in the world remained constant even though it was articulated differently over time in response to changing circumstances. Thus, Brueggemann's understanding of teaching as witness involves not only its formative rootage in Moses, covenant, and Torah but also in an ongoing conversation about morality and in a subversive vision of possibility. Teaching as witness, according to Brueggemann, keeps alive an alternative sense of past, present, and future. It occurs, therefore, in a communal context in which people are invited to share in and reflect upon a particular alternative claim about life, reality, and God. The key pastoral educational issue, in his view, is to consider how to be an apprentice teacher to Moses, including people in a shaping rootage, an ongoing conversation, and a subversive vision.

Samuel Karff discusses the importance of the teaching function within Judaism. The obligations to transmit the heritage from generation to generation and to keep the covenant involve a teaching function that falls primarily to parents, who are to meet the duty in word and example. Karff illustrates how two kinds of Jewish teaching serve this objective: Haggadah, which embodies an understanding of religious truth, and Halakah, which instructs members of the covenant in how to act. Thus, belief and action are prominent within the teaching of Judaism and are considered inseparable. Echoing Brueggemann, Karff observes that Jewish teaching, its interpretation, and its application are subject to change, but any change must be grounded in the heritage. Thus, Jewish teaching is a living tradition with ancient ancestry.

Ritual and observances are means by which Jewish teaching begins during childhood. Parents tell the sacred stories which come alive to children through their active participation in the observances and rituals, including the Bar Mitzvah and Bat Mitzvah ceremonies which integrate children into the full life of the covenant community. The instruction begun during childhood ideally is for faithful Jews an experience of teaching and learning extending through adulthood. A rabbi, according to Karff, is dedicated to a covenant that proclaims the presence and power of God. A primary function of a rabbi is to mediate the Jewish tradition to all the children of Israel. A rabbi, as teacher and priest, is burdened and privileged to be present to people at many of the most teachable moments of life. Thus, rabbis are teachers of Torah to the household of Israel in every setting and in every function.

The communal character of instruction in Judaism is shared by Eastern Orthodox Christianity, according to Stanley Harakas's discussion of Orthodox liturgy. In a manner comparable to Judaism, the past becomes a living presence, and the future is made present in the liturgy. Scripture and tradition are key features of Orthodox worship. Harakas illustrates how they are woven into the fabric of the liturgy and how the liturgy can be a profound and significant educational experience for participants. Orthodox worship, he notes, not only directs the worshiper to God but bears moral and spiritual instruction through hymns and icons. By pointing the worshiper toward God and undertaking the tasks of formation and education, Orthodox liturgy may provide a corrective to certain features of worship in Western Christianity. And, he concedes, certain features of Western Christianity may provide correction to Orthodox Christianity.

Richard McCormick shifts the discussion to a critical examination of the teaching office in the Roman Catholic Church—the magisterium. McCormick argues that the magisterium tends to be misunderstood by Catholics and others. The confusion seems to be stimulated by the contention of some within the Roman Catholic Church that any dissent from noninfallible but authoritative church teaching is disallowed. He contends that this view, which deflates the distinction between infallible and noninfallible teaching, is theologically and historically unsupportable. He considers ordinary teaching, which is subject to correction and change, separate from infallible teaching.

McCormick sees two differing approaches to the magisterium, each embracing a different view of fundamental concepts such as revelation, the function of theology, the role of theologians in academic settings, and models of the church. He believes that while each concept is important, the most critical is the notion of the church.

McCormick illustrates the central role of the notion of the church by examining the idea of *sensus fidelium*, the experience and reflection of the faithful. One view understands the *sensus* as relevant but not determinative: the bishops tell the people what is right. The other view understands the *sensus* as essential: the bishops discover *with* the people what is morally right and wrong. McCormick further illustrates how notions of the church affect the approaches to the magisterium by examining several variables as they were understood before and after the Second Vatican Council. Prior to 1962 these variables generated an understanding that the right to teach was located in a single, hierarchical group in the church, which issued a decisive word. The proper response was obedience or assent. Following 1962, an understanding developed that emphasized learning as a condition for the church's teaching, which was seen as a multidimensional function. The proper response was engagement in the teaching-learning process.

McCormick favors the latter approach in which dissent plays a positive, nonthreatening role in the magisterial function in the church. This openness to a teaching-learning process affects the understanding of the church as teacher by generating a new consciousness about the context, relevant concepts, and components of the magisterium.

McCormick argues that if a participative process of addressing issues of social and personal morality is discontinued, the episcopal magisterium and the papal magisterium will be weakened, theologians will be marginalized, priests will be demoralized, the competence of the laity will be reduced, future ministry will be compromised, and Catholic influence in the world will decline. On this somber note, he concludes with a call to include the entire body of Christ in teaching and the search for truth.

Finally, James Wall reflects on religious teaching outside of the institutional church, that is, as it is reflected in secular media such as cinema and literature. He recalls the film *The Graduate*, in which the central character is offered "plastics," a techno-economic value system, as the basis of a worldview. Against this proposal, Wall argues that the worldview rooted in Jewish and Christian scriptures contains a better value system; but, unlike those who lived when sacred tales in scripture were formed, people today do not seem receptive to the mystery disclosed in this religious worldview and its value system. The sacred worldview that Wall favors does not provide a practical answer to a current problem. Rather, the stories and narratives that convey the sacred worldview offer listeners the possibility of encountering mystery made manifest in the death and resurrection of the Christ.

Wall notes that the gift of mystery awaits acceptance and that it can be conveyed in both religious and secular renderings. An openness to the central story of revelation in religious terms can prepare people to receive further intimations of that same revelation when presented in secular forms. A pastor's task is to tell the sacred story in and through which mystery is encountered. In so doing, pastors and others should realize that the sacred worldview will be disclosed, supplemented, and reinforced in secular forms because revelation is not confined to predictable forms. Burning bushes, says Wall, are everywhere, if recognized and perceived in awe.

Four themes concerning the place and importance of teaching in religious life emerge from these analyses, descriptions, and commentaries. First, the task of religious teaching belongs to the community as a whole and to each of its members. Teaching, like learning, is a lifelong participatory experience that involves all with words and actions. Second, religious teaching embodies a particular perspective on reality and mediates to the learner a distinct identity and vocation. It directs people to another possibility and invites people to share in and reflect upon a particular, alternative truth claim. Third, ritual and liturgy can be rich resources for, and means of, religious instruction, both moral and spiritual. Worship has the potential to unite past, present, and future, pointing the believer toward God and providing moral and spiritual instruction. Fourth, teaching and the search for truth form an evolving quest rooted in the past, conversant with the present, and directed toward the future. The processes of teaching and learning may evoke responsible dissent, which should be viewed constructively as a temporary end to one search and a beginning of another search for new evidence that yields a better answer.

These themes suggest that the segregation of the office of teacher and the task of teaching from other features of the life of religious communities may be attractive organizationally but questionable theologically. This is not to say that specialized ministries that conform to a person's gifts should be rejected. Rather, the essays collectively constitute an implicit call to remember the organic nature of religious belief and life in community—past, present, and future. The duty to teach and learn the sacred story and to relate it to everyday living rests upon everyone. Similarly, every feature of religious life has the potential to be a medium of instruction. If people of faith neglect to transmit the heritage, to be God's instruments of revelation and truth, then the task of calling people to an alternative worldview centered on eternal values will be performed by others in contexts and through media more conducive to God's purposes.

CHAPTER 1

Holy Place, Teaching Place:
The Sanctuary and Education

Maria Harris

WHY DO WE PEOPLE IN CHURCHES SEEM LIKE CHEERFUL, brainless tourists on a packaged tour of the Absolute? . . . On the whole, I do not find Christians, outside the catacombs, sufficiently sensible of conditions. Does anyone have the foggiest idea what sort of power we so blithely invoke? Or as I suspect, does not one believe a word of it? The churches are children playing on the floor with their chemistry sets, mixing up a batch of TNT to kill a Sunday morning. It is madness to wear ladies' straw hats and velvet hats to church; we should be wearing crash helmets. Ushers should issue life preservers and signal flares; they should lash us to our pews. For the sleeping God may wake some day and take offense, or the waking God may draw us out to where we can never return.[1]

So writes Annie Dillard in *Teaching a Stone to Talk*. Is she right? Are we insensible of conditions, and do we realize that explorers unaware of "conditions" have perished? Should we be wearing crash helmets?

In this essay, I am going to side with Dillard. And I am going to talk about conditions—to be specific, five conditions that might shape the sanctuary and the service of worship into a more fitting place for meeting the waking/sleeping God we so blithely invoke. More specifically, I am going to propose that because the sanctuary is a place of mystery, listening, questioning, artistry, and resurrection, we are most true to our work in that place by ministering *through* mystery, listening, questioning, artistry, and resurrection. But before I turn to those five possibilities—those "conditions," as Dillard names them—I must briefly note the educational assumptions I bring.

Educational Assumptions

By using the subtitle "The Sanctuary and Education" in this essay, I do not want to suggest that the sanctuary is primarily a place for educating. I believe it is primarily a place for worshiping God and for proclaiming and interpreting the gospel. But at the same time, and at least secondarily, education is always happening in this setting because of the persons involved and because of the kind of place a sanctuary is. I can clarify that by sharing three presuppositions about the nature of education.

1. *In Christian education, the pastor is not the primary agent of education.* Instead, Christian education is a work where the whole community educates the whole community to live freely, intelligently, and morally in the midst of the world.[2] In such a work, the primary agent is the community, the congregation—present and living, yes—but also the great congregation of the past, the cloud of witnesses sedimented in our life and tradition, most notably the biblical witnesses. And at the heart of the community, at its core at least ideally, is the Holy Spirit. The pastor and others who share the pastoral role are the delegates of this vast congregation and often its most visible representatives, but they are always just that—*representatives* of the larger Body of the Christ. That means that in the sanctuary, the people as a whole educate *through* their pastor, but the people are ultimately responsible.

2. *Education is not equal to schooling.* Most of us would undoubtedly give lip service to this assumption, yet in practice it is remarkable how entrenched the belief is that when we say "education" we are referring to schooling. My point, however, is that the entire life of the church educates in a general way, and each of its ministries educates specifically. We are educated to community and by community; we are educated to outreach and by outreach; we are educated to worship and by worship.[3] These comprise a curriculum of *education*, in contrast to a curriculum of *schooling*,[4] with two powerful implications. First, worship and liturgical life are activities that of themselves are educative; and second, the role of the pastor in such settings is not to be a schoolteacher but presider at worship and a leader of prayer. Although the pastor may act as a schoolteacher at Bible study back in the office or in a classroom, the roles in the sanctuary are different. Those roles are, however, educational.

3. *All institutions teach three curricula: the explicit curriculum, the implicit curriculum, and the null curriculum.*[5] The explicit curriculum is what is consciously offered, what is apparent, what is actually said. The implicit curriculum, in contrast, is what is taught by the forms, the procedures, the patterns; it is what an institution teaches by the kind of place it is and by the way the persons in that place interact with one another.

The null curriculum refers to what is not taught, not offered. The null curriculum is what is left out, whether it be an area of study, a research finding, or a way of going about learning and understanding. The paradox is that the null curriculum exists as a curriculum because it does not exist, because its omissions limit participants in the options they might consider, the perspectives they might employ, and the alternatives they might choose.

In what follows, I will attend mainly to the implicit curriculum—the forms and processes most pertinent to education in the sanctuary—and to the null curriculum—those absent or

unattended conditions that constitute the sanctuary as a holy
place. Examining these conditions (I identify four) as educating forces in the church's life can enable those who are in the
pastoral role to understand how, as they go about their minis-
terial work, education can blossom and then flourish in the
midst of their people. They can recognize the forms of educating propor to the sanctuary. They can learn to ready themselves and their people for the moments when the sleeping
God awakens and the waking God speaks.

The Sanctuary as a Place of Mystery

Mystery is not that about which we cannot know anything;
mystery is that about which we cannot know everything.
Because the focus of life in the sanctuary is the holy Mystery
we call God, at the very least a pastor must never convey in
the sanctuary the idea that we can know everything or that
there are easy answers to life or to death. Instead, mystery is
the reminder that we must always go beyond and outside the
verbal to what, on the one hand, is preverbal, such as silence,
and to what, on the other hand, is supraverbal, such as adoration. In other words, mystery by definition is that which we
can never completely articulate.[6]

But in another rendering, mystery is something in which
we dwell. The philosopher Gabriel Marcel elaborates on this
meaning by distinguishing between a mystery and a problem.
A problem is something I meet that bars my passage and that
is before me in its entirety. It is something I can see, avoid, go
around, or remove. A mystery, however, surrounds and en-
compasses. Instead of something to remove or avoid, it is
something "in which I find myself caught up, and whose
essence is therefore not to be before me in its entirety. It is as
though in this province the distinction between *in me* and
before me loses its meaning."[7] Rudolf Otto approaches the
same reality in his classic *Idea of the Holy* by speaking of
mystery both as *tremendum,* that before which the natural,

human, and appropriate response is awe, and as *fascinans*, that which provokes, fascinates, lures, and draws us in.[8]

In some religious traditions, two further qualifications of mystery appear. In the first, that which has always been understood as the fundamental mystery is God, the Incomprehensible Other who can never be named and who, when felt as possessed, has been by that very feeling lost (e.g., the theology of Karl Rahner). However, because of the Jewish and Christian doctrine of the *Imago Dei*, which teaches that human beings are created in the image of this Incomprehensible Other, the notion of mystery spills over into human life as well. Made in the image of divinity, we too are mysteries.

A second qualification is more central to Christian tradition and is dominant in Roman Catholicism and Orthodoxy, though obviously is not exclusive to them. This is a meaning that comes from the Latin word *sacramentum*, which is itself a translation of the Greek word *musterion*. Although both words have secular meanings, the meaning that has become embedded in Christianity is of a hidden, unseen, profound presence that becomes visible and tangible in persons, in events, and in things. This is the "persistently central assumption that certain objects or actions or words or places belonging to the ordinary spheres of life may convey to us a unique illumination of the whole mystery of our existence, because in these actions and realities . . . something numinous is resident, something holy and gracious." The most revered symbol of this persistent assumption, which Nathan Scott calls the sacramental imagination, is the Christian eucharist.[9]

A final meaning of mystery, found throughout the writings of the apostle Paul (but lost in some translations), is that which links Christ and the Christian (see Eph. 1:7–10; 3:3–6, 14–19; Rom. 6:3–11; 1 Cor. 11:26; Col. 2:11–14; 3:1–4). This tradition reminds us that the dispensation of the fullness of time, where all would be reestablished in the Christ, is the great mystery of the divine will and the focus in our celebration of the Easter "mysteries." And what all of this points toward,

14   MARIA HARRIS

with reference to the sanctuary, is that it is precisely this place, this holy place, this sacred place, this *teaching* place, which provides the opportunity for us to confront mystery. If Paul is right, we do this especially through worship and particularly through the sacred mysteries of baptism and communion. We do it also by providing opportunities for quiet contemplative prayer, when members of the congregation can silently allow themselves to dwell in the mystery who is God. We can help them by celebrating during worship the "negative capability"—the capacity for dwelling in uncertainty and doubt without irritably searching for facts and reasons. We can help by teaching that we must cultivate the powers of waiting and being still—and of not aiming, in the spiritual life, at goals and objectives. We can help by ourselves remembering that the sanctuary is the place created for Sabbath—Sabbath, the time for waiting on the Word and for allowing ourselves to be surrounded by the awesome Shechinah, always there as Companion and Guide.

The Sanctuary as a Place of Listening

Almost necessarily, and in a kind of dynamic rhythm, a second condition emerges from mystery. This is the sanctuary as a place of listening—a place where, as a wise old woman put it, "Sometimes I sets and thinks, and sometimes I jes' sets." Even for the activity of preaching, perhaps especially for the activity of preaching, listening is a prerequisite. For in preaching and interpreting the gospel, the preaching act is at its most genuine when the words are spoken by someone conveying that even as she or he speaks, the words are spilling over from an accompanying attitude of listening.

One of the critical aspects of listening appears in the guise of receptivity, where listening is the activity of disposing oneself to the act of hospitality. Whenever a person enters the sanctuary to preside, the role he or she takes on is that of host.

As hosts, we need to remember that to receive another is not to fill up an emptiness within ourselves with something from outside but rather to help another person participate in a plenitude we are offering.[10] The sanctuary can be such a place when all know they are welcome, when every voice is encouraged, and where those of us who generally inhabit the pulpit invite guests to share it. It is a powerful educative moment when pastors demonstrate regularly that they too are listeners to the word.

This vocation of listening is obviously related to our listening to others and to our capacity to take part in genuine conversation with all in the congregation. Less obvious, but equally important, is the pastoral practice of being receptive to, and listening to, oneself. To me it is self-evident that for a pastor to listen regularly to other persons, there must be a prior and related time set aside to listen to oneself. When Virginia Woolf wrote that a woman needs five hundred pounds a year and a room of her own, the money and the space were symbols of the capacity to receive oneself. To have a room of one's own, a quiet room, a soundproof room, allows us to foster hearing our own heart's song. For such listening, "There must be freedom and there must be peace. Not a wheel must grate, not a light glimmer. The curtains must be close drawn"[11] so that as human beings we may allow ourselves the strength of darkness, the strength of silence. Out of such healing darkness and silence, where we listen to our own deepest mystery, we can learn to listen to one another. One hour a day is not too much time to devote to such spiritual discipline.

Doing that regularly, we can then bring the fruits of listening back to the sanctuary[12] and there do the essential listening proper to the sanctuary—listening to God. That work certainly is the meaning of prayer, since prayer is not so much talking to God as it is listening to God. One who can educate us to the meaning of such listening so that we in turn might

educate others is Nelle Morton, who taught the sacred quality
of listening by describing God as a Great Ear resting at the
heart of the universe. She wrote:

> Once we took the painful journey to the core of our lives, we
> found that we were sustained. In the awful loneliness, we were
> not alone. Something shaped our cry—brought forth our
> speech, fragmentary as it was. We had been told all our lives
> that the word created, that the word came first—even in the
> beginning, before the beginning. Now we know a priority to
> the word—a hearing that brought forth the word. . . . Hearing
> as we have come to experience it, proceeds not from a collec-
> tive ear that would suggest an aggregate, but from a great ear at
> the heart of the universe hearing persons to humanness.[13]

In churches in the United States today, there is one last
form of listening—often part of the null curriculum. This is
our corporate listening, as communities of Christians, to
voices from beyond our own borders, to churches and other
religious bodies around the world, but especially to our near-
est neighbors to the south. Borrowing from John Baptist
Metz, I would call this form of listening "dangerous listening"
because it makes a demand on us.[14] It is a form of listening in
which previously unheard voices break through to the center-
point of our lives and reveal new and dangerous insights for
the present. Such listening illuminates for a few moments and
with a harsh steady light the questionable nature of things we
have apparently come to terms with and shows up the banality
of too much of our ministry. Such listening enables us to
realize that in the helpless other we may discover the sleeping
God, the waiting God, the waking God. In other words, such
listening is prophetic; it challenges us to respond to the lives
of the poor, the unheard, the abused. And it calls us to
consider just how willing we are to face that other meaning of
sanctuary with us today, as demonstrated by communities
who risk their own comfortable security by officially or unof-
ficially becoming a holy place, a sacred place, as they shelter
political refugees who have nowhere to go.

The Sanctuary as a Place of Questioning

The question of providing shelter is precisely that, a question. And it moves us on to a third condition of genuine education in the sanctuary, the sanctuary as a place of questioning. We ought to know that from the Bible, of course, which, far from being the answer to our questions, is much more truly a series of questions to our answers. To confront the incarnate Word, the biblical word, and the human word, as we must in genuine listening, is to move to the realization of just how central questioning is as an element in the church's religious life.

And why is questioning central? To begin with, a question is not only something we pose; it is something we are. Human being is that being in whom being—existence which so often totters on the brink of brokenness and meaninglessness—is always in question; frail, muddled, often sinful human being which nevertheless is situated at the center of the universe. Why are we there at the center? And what demand does that make of us in relation to the rest of creation? Certainly, the sanctuary is the place to raise such questions, especially in the company of the biblical record, the biblical witness.

Following on mystery and on listening, however, the sanctuary becomes critical in the way in which it is either an affirmation of questioning or a haven where questioning is not permitted. It is possible, as we read in Annie Dillard's words, to make the sanctuary a place where questioning is forbidden—a place that suggests that all the data are in on the nature of God, ourselves, and the world. But it is precisely this danger that Annie Dillard rails against—the danger that may cause the sleeping God to awaken suddenly and challenge *us;* question *us.*

What then is possible in the sanctuary as a place of questioning? It seems to me the answer is twofold. First, it is a place for questioning our life *within* the church. Second, it is a place for raising questions about the relation of that "within" life to the surrounding culture beyond the church.

Questioning Within

A phrase that has taken hold of biblical interpretation in our time is the phrase "hermeneutic of suspicion," which describes an attitudinal stance toward scripture and religious teaching. In this stance, a people's present experience is central to raising questions about accepted interpretations of biblical truth. In fact, present experience is held up against interpretation as a kind of measure.[15] In this way of understanding, a community wrestles with a text, just as Jacob wrestled with the angel, in order to find its meaning for contemporary life. A story is told, for example, of Martin Buber reflecting on the fifteenth chapter of the first book of Samuel, in which Saul, having triumphed in battle over the Amalekites, spared their old king, Agag. For that mercy, he was condemned by the prophet Samuel and told he could be king no longer—that that was the will of God. Reflecting on the passage, Buber says that even as a boy, he could not believe that. Buber had come to the conclusion that Samuel had misunderstood God, that Samuel had got God wrong. Such an instance illustrates a hermeneutic of suspicion.[16] In the context of the sanctuary, when a people is gathered, the act of questioning might be carried on in similar fashion. The service must affirm the right, perhaps the duty, to follow Rainer Maria Rilke's counsel:

> Be patient towards all that is unsolved in your heart and try to love the questions themselves like locked rooms. . . . Do not now seek the answers; that cannot be given you because you would not be able to live them. And the point is, to live everything. Live the questions now. Perhaps you will then gradually, without noticing it, live along some distant day into the answer.[17]

Questioning Beyond

This form of questioning was posed recently with great perception by Regis Duffy. Reflecting on the relation of worship beyond the worshiping community, Duffy comments, "There is a striking pastoral dichotomy in our country between the theoretical meanings of [worship] and participants' actions, shaped by their liturgies, in the public sphere where the mission of the church must also be exercised."[18] Out of such commentary, he proposes a set of questions of the kind I am advocating here. The first question is, Does the sanctuary as a place of education have an evangelical impact on the culture that surrounds it? In other words, to what extent has our honest praise of God challenged our own country and its cultural assumptions? Or are our prayer and praise regularly reduced to theological descriptions of the inner life of the individual Christian?

Further, but in the same vein, is Duffy's second question: How does our practice of worship, our life within the sanctuary, provide a sense of direction and of judgment on cultural and religious values outside the sanctuary? Do we continue to use forms that are not fitting to the peoples among whom we live? For example, are we white, Anglo enclaves in the midst of black and Hispanic populations? If so, what and whose values are we implicitly and explicitly celebrating?

And finally, as a "beyond" question: What transformative effect does our worship have in providing and clarifying a sense of mission for our local congregations beyond themselves? If it is true, as a corollary of this question, that any Christian community should be able to be tested by the values and sense of mission it celebrates, the question for each of us here becomes, Does our community do that?[19]

The Sanctuary as a Place of Artistry

With this condition, we come to the most powerful educational aspect of the sanctuary, its use of and its reliance on *form*. Artistry is the creating of form; and in the sanctuary, we pastors need to realize that our artistry educates—or misinforms—through the forms we choose, the designs we employ,

the themes we stress—the *shaping* of the entire situation.
Here, in the condition of artistry, we must attend to John
Dewey's brief remark that the greatest of all pedagogical falla-
cies is the notion that people learn the thing they are studying
at the time. For our purposes, this means that we must be
aware of how powerfully education occurs through the settings, symbols, speech, and sacraments we create in worship—through the implicit curriculum of the sanctuary.

Ideally, the entire congregation enters every service as a
community of creators. Here it is instructive to recall that the
Bible gives us two images of creating.[20] The first is the work of
a maker, a carpenter or a potter, in which something is being
created outside the creator. When the table or pot is finished,
the worker can stand back from it, get distance from it, and
make objective and critical comments about it. The table or
pot is apart; it is separate from the person who created it.

In the second image, however, creating is a brooding,
hovering activity in which the one creating is always within
that which is being created. As the poet Gerard Manley
Hopkins wrote, the Holy Spirit dwells in the midst of the
coming-to-be reality "with warm breast and with ah! bright
wings." In this image, we are never separated from what we
are creating; in this image, the closest analogue is birth. Sings
the Hebrew Bible, "Thou sendest forth thy Spirit, they are
created; and thou renewest the face of the ground" (Ps.
104:30). The Creator God is always present within our individual lives and within our community lives: renewing, energiz-
ing, and recreating.

And so it is with the sanctuary. When people and pastor
come together in that holy place, we are all educated through
the artistry practiced there. As we pastors mold and shape the
activities of worship, we are molded and shaped in return.
And so, as educators in the sanctuary, there are some matters
to which we must attend.

Setting

We pastors need to realize that the physical design of the worship environment, the geography of the sanctuary, can say many things. It can elevate some persons, denigrate others. It can create barriers or invite relation. It can hinder or maximize light. A pulpit strategically placed, for example, can say more about the nature of community and worship in this place than can any other feature of the sanctuary. The choice of flowers, the use of vestments, the display of a flag can also speak volumes. I would counsel everyone to look around the sanctuary at the next visit; observe the teaching it conveys.

Symbols

Some churches use many liturgical symbols: representations of the evangelists, the fish, or the Chi-Rho, for example, may appear in stained glass windows, carved altars, or embroidered vestments. Some use no apparent visual symbols, although the simplicity, the starkness, the absence of visual representation is itself a form of symbolism. But symbolism is also manifest in the gestures and rituals: the ways of conducting communion, the form of the call to worship, the blessings chosen at the end. For example, a service might customarily close with "May the Lord bless and keep thee and give thee peace" or with the Doxology. But on occasion, the symbolism and the educational impact might be changed by closing with the counsel, "The Lord plague thee and torment thee. The Lord set before thee an impossible task, and grant thee the strength to accomplish it. Then and only then, may the Lord grant thee peace."[21]

Speech

Symbolism also educates through speech. I write here not of the message we convey but of the words we choose to frame that message. Emily Dickinson's advice is pertinent here:

"Tell the truth, but tell it slant." We can do that if we develop
a repertoire of forms in which to shape our message: narrative
that investigates reality through story; myth that establishes
the nature of reality by drawing on archetypal figures; parable
that subverts reality by providing the puzzling ending or the
one we resist, thereby giving God room and shattering the
structural security of the listeners' expectations.[22] And song is
symbolic: song from the choir and song from the preacher;
song where the entire congregation stands and celebrates;
song that is antiphonal between choir and congregation; and
song that comes from the southern, western, northern, and
eastern peoples of our world, challenging our artistry and
opening it to new possibilities.

Sacrament

Finally, we need to attend to the great artistic forms of ritual
and sacramental ceremony. After suffering a stroke, Reinhold
Niebuhr rethought much of his earlier perspective on sacramental worship as he moved from pulpit to pew for the
remaining twelve years of his life. He describes the experience:

> As I became a pew-worshiper rather than the preacher, I had
> some doubts about the ability of us preachers to explicate and
> symbolize the majesty and mystery. These pulpit-centered
> churches of ours, without a prominent altar, seemed insuffi-
> cient. . . . I came to view the Catholic mass as, in many
> respects, more adequate than our Protestant worship. For the
> first time I ceased to look at Catholicism as a remnant of
> medieval culture. I realized that I envied the popular Catholic
> mass because the liturgy, for many, expressed the mystery
> which makes sense out of life always threatened by mean-
> inglessness.[23]

Should Niebuhr's confession resonate in our spirits, it may be
time to reclaim our own powers of artistry and reshape the

ceremonial dimensions of our worship so that ritual and sacrament are reclaimed as a possession of all Christian people.

The Sanctuary as a Place of Resurrection

Even in the midst of December, Christians are an Easter people. Augustine is credited with the suggestion that every Christian is to be an alleluia from head to foot. The sanctuary is a place where people are called to be together on a day of the week that commemorates resurrection. The original and sustaining impulse for coming to the sanctuary—whenever that happens—is to hear the good news of rebirth and resurrection. As a final condition, then, resurrection teaches us the completion of education in the sanctuary, reminding us of the basic truth that makes this forever a holy place, a teaching place. How might this be so?

To begin with, a focus on resurrection is a focus on Jesus, the Christ, who is risen, and on the risen Christ, who in the divine person as well as in his embodied humanity points to God. The focus is on the one who became human, suffered, and died—the one who did not distribute solutions to problems but who came and lived human life to the end, calling us to do the same. The point here is that from the beginning, the focus of the Gospels is the cry "The Lord is risen." The focus of the Gospels is an assertion about God before it is a puzzling reported fact about Jesus. The focus is *not* on a doctrine or its meaning or analysis.

The implications for our life together in the sanctuary ought to be clear. Our life together, when we gather as *koinonia,* is not to analyze and theologize: it is to proclaim, over and over, the good news that although death and brokenness abound, grace and God abound even more. The risen Christ is God promising, "I am; I am here. And I will never forsake you." The risen Christ is God answering our plea, "Don't talk to me, don't question me, don't touch me. Stay with me."

Resurrection also exists as a condition describing the present, not just the past. It is a reminder of the question of what the risen Christ means to us now; it is similar to the situation we meet at Christmas. For just as there is no baby Jesus now, so there is no crucified Jesus now. Lent is not a time for pretending that Easter is *coming;* it is the affirmation that *now,* and in all the church seasons of our gathered lives, there is only the transformed, glorious, and immortal divine–human person, the Christ, who has conquered sin and death and is the living head of the church, the living head of the mystical body. The Christ has not retired from the world, leaving divine truths behind. Instead, the living Christ is forever with us, in us, and among us.

This is a message often missed, although the authors of scripture are at pains to point out that their intention is not to describe a dead past but to say, "Look. See what God is doing now, in your present lives." The implications for education in the sanctuary would appear to be that there, in that place, we attempt to speak and live similarly, with a focus on the present.

In addition, resurrection as present reality offers us an imagery. For the life of worship is not so much an activity of going up, as in worsh-up, as it is of going down and toward the present depths of our present lives, toward the center. *"Descendit ad inferos,"* often understood as "He descended into hell," is better understood as a positive statement, affirming a deeper and deeper movement of conversion. For our journey toward God is not toward a top; it is a journey toward a center.

Resurrection is also an affirmation of "bodiliness." The resurrection texts, for example, are remarkable in their stress on food, eating, and touching, with Jesus preparing the meal and revealing himself in the breaking of bread. As such they remind us that our religious lives are not a call to immortality of the soul, where the body is ultimately not significant. Instead, it is a call to the affirmation of bodiliness and to the personal, social, and historical character of human reality.

In the sanctuary, that will mean a check and a guard on any piety that is centered on a life after death or that denies the bodiliness of our human selves. It will also mean we pastors must attend to all those sensible realities that feed the body: from the bread and wine of communion, to the potluck supper afterward, to the color and design of banners, to the pleasing perfume of incense which affirms a God who had made all things good.

And finally, the resurrection, for Christians, is a condition saying something about the world. Some Christians hold that the resurrection means that although Jesus died, he still lives on in the faith of his followers. But a deeper affirmation is that the reality called resurrection is a *cosmic* event. It is a way of saying that God is present to the entire world, whether people are Christians or not. This means that in resurrection—and therefore in the sanctuary—we Christians do not celebrate the founding of a church. We celebrate the re-creation of a world. Because of the risen Christ, the world is different. And though the peoples of other religious traditions may have similar and complementary symbols, this one is ours to affirm and to cherish.

Resurrection says the world is different. But it is not yet whole; it is not yet healed. That is the work left for us to do. And so even as we celebrate resurrection in our own sanctuaries, we may want to imitate a ritual in the Passover Haggadah.[24] At the Seder service, the cup of thanksgiving is passed around the table to rejoice over the escape of the Hebrews from bondage in Egypt. Before the second of four cups is shared, however, each person removes from the cup, with the tip of a finger, ten drops of wine, which will not be drunk. They are dropped onto a plate and carried away from the table, because each drop represents a plague visited upon Egypt before Pharaoh let the Hebrews go.

Because our freedom was gained at the price of their hunger, disease, and death of their firstborn, the cup of thanksgiving cannot be full. We mourn that our liberty was gained through their suffering and our happiness is not complete.[25]

So it is with us Christians. The resurrection has happened, and because of it our world is different. But while we are living in the midst of suffering and hunger, pain and oppression, that world is not yet complete. A sacred and holy attending to education in the sanctuary, however, could bring us to a place where the incompleteness is lessened. Then, should the sleeping God awake or the waking God draw us forth, we might walk without fear. For we have celebrated *in* mystery, *through* listening and questioning, *with* artistry, and *out* of the hope of resurrection. Possibly, we can do no more. Certainly, we can do no less.

Notes

1. Annie Dillard, *Teaching a Stone to Talk* (San Francisco: Harper & Row, 1982), 40.
2. See Gabriel Moran, *Religious Body* (New York: Seabury Press, 1974), 150ff., for development of this assumption.
3. See Maria Harris, *Portrait of Youth Ministry* (Paramus, N.J.: Paulist/Newman Press, 1981).
4. See Gabriel Moran, *Religious Education Development* (Minneapolis: Winston Press, 1983), chap. 8, for the distinction between the curriculum of education and the curriculum of schooling.
5. Elliot Eisner, *The Educational Imagination*, 2d ed. (New York: Macmillan Co., 1985), 87–108. The null curriculum corresponds to what some educators call "excluded knowledge."
6. See Maria Harris, *Teaching and Religious Imagination* (San Francisco: Harper & Row, 1987), 13–14.
7. Gabriel Marcel, *Being and Having* (Boston: Beacon Press, 1951), 27–28.
8. Rudolf Otto, *The Idea of the Holy* (New York: Oxford University Press, 1950), 1–40.

9. Nathan Scott, *The Wild Prayer of Longing* (New Haven: Yale University Press, 1971), 49.
10. Gabriel Marcel, *Creative Fidelity* (New York: Farrar, Straus & Giroux, 1964), 28.
11. Virginia Woolf, *A Room of One's Own* (New York: Harcourt Brace Jovanovich, 1957), 182.
12. This idea is built on the ancient phrase *Contemplata aliis tradere*, which is translated into English as "The fruits of contemplation are to be handed on to others."
13. Nelle Morton, "The Dilemma of Celebration," in *Womanspirit Rising*, ed. Carol Christ and Judith Plaskow (New York: Harper & Row, 1979), 164–65.
14. See John Baptist Metz, *Faith in History and Society* (New York: Seabury Press, 1980), 109–10, for an explication of dangerous memory, from which this section is derived.
15. Paul Ricoeur is associated with the first use of the idea of a hermeneutic of suspicion. In liberation theology, it is the basis of the "hermeneutic circle." See Juan Luis Segundo, *The Liberation of Theology* (Maryknoll, N.Y.: Orbis Books, 1976), 7–39.
16. Martin Buber, "Autobiographical Fragments," in *The Philosophy of Martin Buber*, ed. Paul Arthur Schelpp and Maurice Friedman (La Salle, Ill.: Open Court, 1967), 31–32.
17. Rainer Maria Rilke, *Letters to a Young Poet* (New York: W. W. Norton, 1934), 33.
18. Regis Duffy, "The U.S. Catholic Contribution to Liturgy," *New Theology Review* 1, no. 1 (February 1988): 31.
19. Ibid., 31–52.
20. John V. Taylor, *The Go Between God: The Holy Spirit and the Christian Mission* (Philadelphia: Fortress Press, 1973), 25ff.
21. A suggestion made in an unpublished paper of Ann Johnson. Newton Centre, Massachusetts, 1986.
22. See John Dominic Crossan, *The Dark Interval* (Niles, Ill.: Argus Communications, 1976), chap. 1, for development of forms of word and speech.
23. Reinhold Niebuhr, "A View from the Sidelines," *Christian Century* 101 (Dec. 19–26, 1984), 1195–98.
24. Leslie Simonson in an unpublished paper. Boston, 1982.
25. Passover Haggadah. Compiled by the Area Jewish Group of Concord, Massachusetts, April 1982. Pesach 5742, p. 6.

CHAPTER 2

Teaching as Witness:
Forming an Intentional Community

Walter Brueggemann

THE TEACHING OFFICE AND TEACHING INSTITUTION IN AN-
cient Israel are elusive and difficult to identify.[1] The teaching
function, however, is much more visible and pervasive. The
Old Testament is saturated with teachers and teaching. There
is enormous variety and variation; but there is, in a broad
sense, an identifiable commonality about that teaching enterprise. Everywhere and in all cases, this teaching is a convinced, passionate, partisan activity that urges a particular
perspective on reality and that mediates to the learner a
distinct identity and vocation.[2] That is, teaching is aimed at
the creation of a particular community of discernment and
practice. This teaching is always ready to differentiate itself
from other perspectives and other discernments that it judges
to be false, foolish, or death dealing. Being in a mode that is
partisan, passionate, and potentially polemical, this teaching
is indeed a witness. It bears witness to a particular truth
claim, to the exclusion of other truth claims.[3]

"Witness" is characteristically not practiced to support a
dominant ideology. It is neither necessary nor appropriate for

28

that purpose. Witness is characteristically the articulation of an alternative that is perceived from the viewpoint of dominant ideology as not only alternative but also as subversive.

The Witness of Moses

Moses occupies the central teaching office and the decisive teaching function in the Old Testament. He is the figure from which all other teaching derives in ancient Israel. The episode of the burning bush (Exod. 3:1–6) is the foundational event that authorizes and energizes Moses to create a community that is an intentional alternative to the Egyptian empire. Moses' teaching is to witness that an alternative is mandated by God and is politically possible in the real world.

The teaching function of Moses is to teach the *liberation* of Exodus, the *covenant* of Sinai, and the *fulfillment* of the promise of land. Moses' teaching is, of course, by praxis. That is, Moses does not simply talk about these matters but he shows Israel how to be free, bound in covenant, and landed. His life work is the authorization of radical and bold activity on the part of Israel to distance and distinguish itself theologically, politically, economically, and geographically from the modes, assumptions, and claims of the Egyptian empire.

Gerhard von Rad[4] and, following him, Norman K. Gottwald[5] have shown how the two pivotal events of Exodus from Egypt ("going out") and entering the land of Canaan ("coming in") set the limits and extreme claims of Israel's life and Moses' teaching. Everything has to do with "He brought us out; he brought us in." From the beginning, Moses bears witness that Israel's alternative life consists of leaving the empire, receiving the gift, and ordering its life in a new kind of way.

The Exodus tradition is witness to the revolutionary fact that Israel's life is not intended to be one of endless submission to imperial reality. Moses, by organization, political courage, and liturgical enactment, teaches Israel *ressentiment*, permits Israel to touch the deep hurt of oppression, generates

social criticism of the empire which by criticism is delegiti-
mated, and so releases in Israel the social imagination to
dream of and hope for the world in a different way.[6] At Sinai,
Moses bears witness that there is another sovereign who
displaces imperial sovereignty, whose bondage is real freedom, whose freedom is demanding obedience.[7] At the door of
the new land, Moses teaches (at length in Deuteronomy) of
the wonders of the new land, of well-being, and of the risks of
seduction and distortion awaiting Israel in the land of Canaan.
Moses' credo recital of Exodus and land communicates in
Israel the awareness that Israel has a peculiar way in the
world, a peculiar burden, and a peculiar possibility that must
not be compromised. For if Israel compromises, it will "surely
perish" (Deut. 8:19–20). That is, if Israel does not hold to its
radical vision and radical practice, it will disappear and its
people will once more be submissive to the empire.

Out of this credo, which is recited relentlessly in all kinds of
variations as the core witness of Israel,[8] has come Israel's
foundational literature, the Torah. Von Rad has shown how
these five scrolls, the Pentateuch, are in fact an extended
exposition of Israel's core credo.[9] Gottwald has shown how
this extended literature is not simply a residue of memory but
a literature that continues, in every generation, to give impe-
tus for revolutionary activity in the world.[10] Moses did not
write that entire literature, but this originary teacher provided the status and *hutzpah* to continued exposition of the
core claim. After Moses, others continued to state, restate,
and state again in fresh ways for fresh circumstances that
Israel's way in the world is distinctive because of its summons
from this distinctive God. In the end, it is not the voice of
Moses but the dangerous witness of this text that is Israel's
true and decisive teacher. The Torah tradition mediates the
"strange new world within the Bible."[11] It is so strange, not
because of peculiar myths or odd laws, but because it asserts
that there is another membership available that permits dis-

engagement from the dominant membership in the empire.[12] One need not submit to the dominant membership!

It is this strange witness rooted in the Book of Exodus but extrapolated all over the Pentateuch to which Israel has repeated recourse. In the end, Israel really has nothing else to teach its children except to bear witness to this subversive memory and to make the case that this odd alternative continues to be viable and valid in every circumstance, even where it is unwelcome and alien.

Six times the traditions of Moses and Joshua urge this memory as the core of teaching testimony:[13]

And when your children say to you, "What do you mean by this service?" you shall say . . . (Exod. 12:26–27).

And you shall tell your son on that day, "It is because . . . (Exod. 13:8).

And when in time to come your son asks you, "What does this mean?" you shall say to him . . . (Exod. 13:14).

When your son asks you in time to come, "What is the meaning of the testimonies and the statutes and the ordinances which the LORD our God has commanded you?" then you shall say . . . (Deut. 6:20–21).

. . . that this may be a sign among you, when your children ask in time to come, "What do these stones mean to you?" Then you shall tell them . . . (Josh. 4:6–7).

When your children ask their fathers in time to come, "What do these stones mean?" then you shall let your children know . . . (Josh. 4:21–22).

These references have some variation. But in general, we may note certain recurring dimensions:

1. These were real events that happened. The events are knowable and identifiable. There is content to be known.

32   WALTER BRUEGGEMANN

2. These events concern the reality and activity of God, who is embarrassingly an active partner in the narrative.
3. These events concern us and they concern "you." They are not events that Israel's children have outgrown or will outgrow. These events are definitional for us all.
4. These events have radical, contemporary, life-identifying implications. They continue to be valid, and they continue to apply to real events, decisions, and issues, permitting and requiring a particular field of discernment.

The purpose of this testimonial instruction is to include the next generation in this partisan, passionate, polemical practice of reality.

In the completed Pentateuch, the writer "Moses" has lingered longest over the Sinai events, extending the obligations of covenant through the Books of Exodus and Leviticus and much of Numbers and Deuteronomy. This material is at the center of the literature, placed between the Exodus and the entry into the land. In the finished literature, the teaching focus is on an alternative obedience. It asks, How is this people to live in covenant with the liberating God? The answer is, By doing the will of the new sovereign.

It is impossible and presumptuous to "summarize" the substance of obedience required in the Torah. We may, however, identify two tendencies in this tradition of ethical discourse. On the one hand, the will of Yahweh, the inscrutable actor in this narrative, is for *justice*, for the practice of redemptive, healing equity that assures every member of the community an adequate share of life-space, life-goods, and life-power. Characteristically, this guarantee of life is extended to every member of the community, especially the marginal. Special care is taken that the distribution of life-goods should not be skewed under the pressure of power and privilege. Indeed, the Israelite is instructed in a mandate of justice precisely to resist the seductions of power and privilege.[14]

On the other hand, and perhaps this is more elemental than is justice, Israel ponders a *vocation of holiness*. To be a holy people living in intense communion with a holy God, Israel has understood that this God is inaccessible and unapproachable. To dare to live in communion with this God is an awesome, risky enterprise. Israel may draw close but must not presume. Israel must not presume to penetrate the mystery of God, to domesticate the source of life, to preempt the powers of governance. To live in this awkward, privileged danger, Moses devises careful provisions and regulations that sort out what is possible and permissible. The process of sorting out inducts Israel into a holy destiny of being God's special, valued partner through its life in the world. While the matter is never precisely articulated, Moses proposes to Israel that *holiness* in relation to God and *justice* in relation to neighbor are intimately related and delicately, dialectically dependent on each other.

The long poem of Deuteronomy 32, the Song of Moses, may be taken as the epitome of Moses' work as a teacher who witnesses. The poem is judged to be very old, and it no doubt articulates the central matters of Mosaic faith.[15] Moreover, it is placed in the Pentateuchal literature very close to the death of Moses and the transition to the subsequent leadership of Joshua. The poem begins with the statement of "my teaching" (v. 2), which is judged to be as life-giving as rain. Israel lives by the teaching of Moses even as the grass lives by rain—and cannot live without it.

The first part of the poem, a lawsuit speech, is in three parts. Verses 10–14 narrate God's initial graciousness to Israel by reviewing the canonical memory. Verses 15–18 tell of Israel's stubbornness, resistance, and refusal to be Yahweh's special, obedient people. Finally, vv. 19–33 contain a long statement about God's destructive judgment on this recalcitrant people. This long section asserts that the covenant relation is morally serious and morally dangerous. Yahweh is inordinately gracious but will not be mocked. In the end, Israel must come to terms with Yahweh on Yahweh's terms. There is no alternative. This is single-option existence. On any other terms, the covenant dissolves and Israel ceases to exist. Israel's special vocation is forfeited, and the social alternative of covenant is nullified. Mosaic testimony is clear and as harsh as the subject required.

George Ernest Wright has seen, however, that at v. 39 there is a curious break in the poem.[16] Now the abrasion of moral violation is superseded, and Yahweh asserts a new compassion and a new vindication for Israel, the old violation not withstanding (v. 36). In this section of the poem, Yahweh is portrayed as so committed to Israel that the obstinateness and anger just articulated are now bracketed out. Yahweh will intervene in behalf of Israel.

The two sections of this poem that epitomize Mosaic teaching contain a fundamental contradiction. On the one hand, there is a quid pro quo of moral earnestness to which Israel, at great risk, must subscribe. On the other hand, there is an action of Yahweh (not measured or bound by this moral structure) that enacts Yahweh's yearning out beyond moral qualification. This contradiction is found not only in the poem but throughout the literature and surely in the very heart of God.[17] Israel has discerned that because of this contradiction the exactitudes of imperial requirement are not the last word. There is slippage in reality that is intentional, not accidental or careless. This slippage permits healing and the breaking of deathly cycles.

If this poem had ended with v. 38, it would conform to the uncompromising demands of the empire. It runs beyond empirelike demands, however, to the yearning resolve of Yahweh. Israel has at its center a conviction of destabilization that deabsolutizes every claim of ultimacy for every concentration of royal power. There is a beginning again in God's resolve, so that the Song of Moses ends on a note of triumphant, inexplicable hope. That hope is articulated in the face of imperial reality, which is always hopeless in its conformity and reductionism. It is the freedom of Yahweh to act in compassion and vindication that breaks the grip of every formulation of competence. How strange to hear this on the lips of Moses, who has spent so much energy on the demands of the Torah!

Later Witnesses

Moses the teacher died (Deut. 34:5–8). But of course, as the water gives life to the grass, so the subversive teaching of Moses survived and continued to nourish and give life to Israel. The teaching survived the teacher. Indeed, the power and vitality of the teaching recruited other teachers. We may identify three modes in which the alternative witness of Moses continued.

Joshua and Samuel

The two great mediators, Joshua and Samuel, surely continue the Mosaic function and seek to induct new generations of Israel into this peculiar covenant-based, Torah-oriented practice of life. Joshua is presented as the proper successor to Moses.[18] In Joshua 24, a much studied chapter, Joshua performs again the Mosaic function of covenant formation, authorizing an alternative community. Joshua retells the long Torah narrative (vv. 2–13), and then he summons Israel to decide for the peculiar vision of Yahwism and against the conventions of their environment.

> Now therefore fear the LORD, and serve him in sincerity and in faithfulness; put away the gods which your fathers served. . . . Choose this day whom you will serve (Josh. 24:14–15).

The choice of a certain God is the embrace of a specific teaching and acceptance of a specific destiny and vocation in the world. To adhere to Yahweh is to forsake other gods, other ethics, other life practices. As Joshua has been bearing witness in the tradition of Moses, so now the responsive Israelites agree to be witnesses to the awesome decision and the costly loyalty they have embraced (v. 22). Israel is again set on a course of alternative life.

The same transaction is executed by Samuel in a later generation. Samuel is party to an enigmatic debate about the proper character of the community. The topic is kingship. The issue, however, is the sovereignty of Yahweh and the shape of public power. Finally Israel agrees to have a human king, a decision perceived by some as a serious departure from the Sinai affirmation of Yahweh's kingship. In a great convocation, Samuel teaches Israel about its peculiar life in the world (1 Samuel 12). He echoes Moses at Sinai and Joshua at Shechem.[19] He reviews Israel's history with Yahweh (vv. 7–12) and insists that the old forms of power and prayer are still valid (vv. 17–18). It is most interesting that in vv. 14, 15, and 25 Samuel completely subordinates the new king to the old covenantal requirements of the Torah. In the face of obedience to the Torah, the king (an experiment of human assertion) is reckoned like anyone else who must submit to the peculiar tradition of covenantal demand. In the central section, vv. 14–15, Samuel reduces the political possibility of Israel to the covenantal formulation of "if . . . then," presenting exactly the same structure that Moses did in Deuteronomy 32. Joshua and Samuel insist, like Moses, that freedom in bondage to Yahweh is a viable way to live one's life in the world. Samuel's teaching is an insistence that public power and historical possibility have a non-negotiable moral shape which must be honored.

The Levites

The Levites are a difficult and obscure presence in Israel. But they must be regarded in a peculiar way as the primary bearers of the Mosaic tradition. They are the priestly group not so smitten with God's static, cultic presence. Instead they insist that Israel's life is ordered around the radicalness of the

Torah. In Deut. 33:8–11, Moses entrusts to the Levites the office of instruction in the Torah. It is the Levites who have faithfully kept the covenant (v. 9) and who are to instruct Israel. The Levites embody the continued tradition of the most radical Mosaic teaching, a teaching that resists both the domestication of the monarchy and the "detoxification" that was sponsored by the temple priesthood.

Three scholarly hypotheses support this continued and radical tradition: (1) a number of scholars follow von Rad in locating the egalitarian teaching of Deuteronomy among the Levites;[20] (2) Hans Walter Wolff has proposed that the radical covenant teaching of Hosea is derived from and reflective of the ongoing Levitical teaching;[21] (3) Gottwald has proposed that the Levites are a "revolutionary cadre" in Israel who fostered Moses' conviction of a radical egalitarian social alternative.[22] The witness of this tradition is that the dominant imperial perception of reality is not absolute.

The Prophets

There is no doubt that the great prophets of the eighth and seventh centuries continue the Mosaic paradigm. Scholars are now nervous and cautious about claiming too close a connection, and perhaps it has been overstated. The conclusion seems unavoidable, however, that the prophets draw on the old ethical tradition of the Torah and that the form of lawsuit speech is a direct derivative from the notion of stipulation and curse in the covenant.[23] Against the various temptations of palace and temple, of greedy capitalism, exaggerated nationalism, and seductive naturalism, the prophets bore witness to a covenantal perception of reality rooted in the Torah. On the one hand, Hosea and Jeremiah especially make repeated appeal to the old saving events as the ground from which to perceive the world differently. On the other hand, they insist that there is moral answerability to Yahweh.

Even when the terrible ending of 587 B.C.E. came, the

great voices of hope in exile (Jeremiah, Ezekiel, and especially Isaiah 40–55) continue to appeal to the same tradition.[24] While the lawsuit formulation had been vindicated and had run its course in 587, the imaginers of a new possibility pressed deeper into the tradition and found again a God who is capable of a fresh, originary act that permits Israel to reemerge. Now the stress is not on moral coherence but on the capacity for a *novum*, a newness articulated by Moses at the end of Deuteronomy 32. While this God takes moral formulations seriously, they are not taken with ultimate seriousness. More decisive than moral requirement is the capacity and will of Yahweh to break the cycles of death and begin again. Through all these long centuries, the great mediators, the Levites, and the prophets in various ways insisted that Moses had it right.

The Witnessing Teachers of the Exile

The Mosaic formulation of reality, however, was not by itself adequate. The events of 587, with the loss of temple, monarchy, and political identity, created a deep theological crisis for Israel. Neither the moral coherence of Moses (Sinai) nor the capacity for a *novum* (Exodus) could any longer be presented in the old way with the old confidence. Israel, of course, continued to look to Moses. Even the Mosaic claims required inventive reformulation. The witnessing teachers of Israel can never simply reiterate; they must find fresh ways of articulation.

There is, in this moment of displacement, a massive shift of paradigm in Israel's self-discernment. The canonical events of Exodus, Sinai, and entrance into the land are now displaced in urgency. Now Israel must speak of exile and, if possible, restoration. To be sure, exile-restoration is not uncongenial to the Mosaic pattern of liberation-covenant, but it is not the same. The Mosaic conviction of covenantal accountability could almost account for exile in terms of disobedience, but the exile is not fully accommodated to simple moral categories of requirement and sanction. There is a surplus of dread and rage that is more than proper punishment. The theme of return and restoration, moreover, is not unlike the liberation of Exodus (cf. Jer. 23:7–8), but the return from exile seems more unlikely and odd in its happening, as perceived in the sixth century B.C.E.

The great witnessing teachers of the exile thus are required to do enormously inventive interpretation.[25] They utilized old memories; but they submitted the old memories to the rawness of present experience, to the deep shame and dread of displacement, and to the shabby, modest wonder of restoration, which was happening only a little and only a little at a time.

In the process of this remarkable reinterpretation, the focus of Israel's self-understanding and self-interpretation shifts. Now Israel has a fresh consciousness of the dread of chaos, of the reality of historical nullification and cosmic "not-being," of the radicalness of newness and the inexplicable surprise of *creatio ex nihilo* (cf. Isa. 45:18–19). Israel's experience pushed Israel's language and imagination outside the frame of historical experience and explanation. Now Israel's witness concerns something more dark and inscrutable, and more wondrous than the old memory seemed to offer.

Jacob Neusner is most helpful in discerning what happened.[26] It is clear that not all the people of Judah were carried away. Clearly not all those carried away came home. The homecoming is less glorious, even less identifiable, than we are led to believe. The model of "exile-restoration" is not a flat descriptive report of what happened. It is, rather, an imaginative construction wrought out of experience but shaped by the imaginative, interpretive portrayal of poets who imposed their rendering on historical facts.[27] These teachers insisted that it is this reading of reality (and not some other) that is correct. They were able to entertain the void between displacement and restoration, to live with the dread idea that

Israel for a moment did not exist, and, then, that Israel, by the power of sovereign holiness, was convened again.

This witness asserted how precarious Israel is, how blessed, how treasured, and how grateful Israel must be, how astonished to exist rather than to have ceased to be. Neusner puts it this way: "Judaism took shape as the system that accounted for the death and resurrection of Israel, the Jewish people, and pointed for the source of renewed life toward sanctification now, and salvation at the end of time."[28] He takes up the language of death and resurrection, of alienation and reconciliation, to articulate the identity of Jews as one of marginality, precariousness, and living on borrowed, grateful time. Israel knows that it will never drive out the anguish of death or the pain of alienation, the terrible restlessness that keeps the community under way and at risk. All of this Moses had inchoately understood.

Now, however, this restlessness and anguish are fixed as normative and generative. It is this restlessness for "salvation at the end of time" that makes Judaism hopeful for what is to come and, finally, resistant to being administered in every present time. It is this fragility and astonishment that drives Israel to endless reflection on its character and identity, aware that its identity is not like others, cannot conform to others, but is an odd destiny marked by moral seriousness; it is open to dream and to trembling, as other nations are not. Israel teaches its young to dream always about new homecoming and reconciliation. Israel teaches its young to tremble before the power of the Holy One who can take up permanent habitation with any other or with us. The generative model of social identity required by the exile broke the Mosaic synthesis and evoked a variety of teaching witnesses.

The Forms of the Teaching Witness

In the postexilic, postrestoration period of the Old Testament, the period when Judaism received its decisive casting, the teaching function took a variety of forms.[29] Here I shall mention three that I believe are important for understanding Judaism's witness to itself and to the Gentiles: the work of Ezra the scribe, the witness of the wisdom teachers, and the witness of the apocalyptic.

The Witness of Ezra the Scribe

The first and preeminent form of teaching is the work of Ezra the scribe. The restoration of Judaism under Ezra and Nehemiah is riddled with historical problems.[30] What is clear is that somewhere in the fifth century B.C.E. there was a concerted effort by zealous Jews returned from exile, who had Persian authorization, to reestablish the foundations of Judaism. While there may have been other efforts, it is this one that "stuck" and became canonical, establishing the decisive shape of the Jewish community.

The great text, reckoned as crucial as the meeting at Sinai, is Nehemiah 8. In that text Ezra the scribe assembles all the people in Jerusalem for the reading of "the book of the torah of Moses." *Ezra reads Moses.* Judaism returns to the old tradition. The recovery of faith, the reordering of the community, begins with a return to the old tradition. All the people listened attentively. It was the Levites who helped the people understand by interpreting, so that the old text was made pertinent to the current situation. It is noteworthy that it was the Levites, carriers of the Mosaic memory, who did the exegesis. The people understood as the Levites understood, and they again constituted Israel.[31] The Torah, the Levites, the interpretation, the scribe all bore partisan witness concerning what it meant and means to be a distinct people. In this moment Judaism is shaped again as a coherent force that will convene a community.

I want to identify three derivations from that interpretive act of reconstitution. First, the Jews are admonished not to grieve (Neh. 8:9–11), but to hold a feast of joy. They celebrate the Festival of Booths, and in doing so they replicate and enter into the old memory of God's joyous presence. This joyous festival is an alternative to their propensity to grieve. Presumably Jews have much to grieve over. They are in a shabby situation near to despair. Their teachers nonetheless instruct them to an alternative act of joy. An act of joy rooted in the tradition is to counter the grief evoked by circumstance. The community is not to be shaped by circumstance but to act in the world accountable to its own sense of self, fed by sacramental imagination. The Festival of Booths is an act of defiance against a more natural grief. These Jews are not to succumb to their environment.

Second, in Nehemiah 9 the Levites lead the Jews in an extended liturgy. They begin by separating themselves from all foreigners (9:2). That is, they gather, mindful of their peculiar destiny as the people of the Exodus and the covenant, of exile and restoration. Ezra prays. (It is a long prayer, long because Ezra recites the whole narrative memory of Israel.) One motif in the recital is Israel's guilt, which is not covered over or denied. Judaism does not imagine it can slough off or deny its looming past. The powerful rhetoric of the prayer, however, does not linger over guilt. The crucial element is "*thou*." Ezra's world is peopled with a partner. Israel has someone to address. Israel knows to whom it prays. Israel prays to the one with whom it has a long history. It is "thou, thou, thou" who overrides Israel's guilt.

Israel prays with exile on its heart. Verses 17–19, appealing to the old tradition, meditate on the verb *forsake*. "Thou didst not forsake." The prayer is addressed to this one who is utterly reliable. No, God is more than reliable. The most frequent and reliable word is *mercy:* "according to thy great mercies" (v. 27; cf. vv. 28, 31). Israel's world is surrounded by a "thou" who does not forsake and who is merciful. Israel lives in the reality made available by the remembered tradition.

In the end, the prayer takes a noteworthy turn. It does not escape into memory but stays close to today.

Behold, we are slaves this day; in the land that thou gavest to our fathers to enjoy its fruit . . . behold, we are slaves. And its rich yield goes to the kings whom thou hast set over us because of our sins; . . . we are in great distress (vv. 36–37).

Israel's prayer, like Israel's perceptual field, can never stay away from public realities for long, especially from economic realities. All the talk of sin and mercy finally gets to the immediate case. Israel prays to the God of liberation and reconciliation because in this moment it yearns for liberation and homecoming. The remembered tradition turns resentful yearning into urgent, confrontive hope. Israel's restlessness does not settle for how the world presently is.

The third derivation, in Nehemiah 5, is a crucial and much-neglected text. The subject is economic oppression, the same subject that is found at the end of the prayer in chapter 9. In chapter 9 the oppression is linked to a foreign king. Here in chapter 5 the problem is internal oppression, Jew against Jew. In both cases the issue is economic justice. Why should some be subservient to others at risk of their lives? Here there is no religious talk, but talk of mortgages and taxes. Some have been forced to borrow to pay the king's tax. While it is spoken of as the king's tax, the Persians must have had Jewish functionaries, because the outcry is against "Jewish brethren."

Nehemiah hears and is enraged. He is capable of wondrous social indignation because he is a child of the memory of egalitarianism. Nehemiah chides and rebukes the profiteers. He advises that interest on debts be cancelled and mortgaged property be returned. There is an agreement. Nehemiah's proposal is accepted. The financial crisis is resolved because appeal has been made to the covenantal character of communal life, which exploitive interest violates.

These texts can be read at two levels. First, for the contemporaries of Nehemiah, the old memories of Deuteronomy prohibiting interest exercised compelling authority, and they caused changed behavior (cf. Deut. 23:19). Second, the events of Nehemiah now become an instructional text itself to bear witness to subsequent generations about the practice of alternative economics.

On three counts, the witness of Ezra-Nehemiah grows out of the memory of the Torah: *joy*, in the face of grief as a defiant sacramental act; *prayer* for mercy based on the history of God's mercy; and *economic reform* based on communal identity and the requirement of the Torah.

Finally, we observe that in Neh. 8:4–7 and 9:4–5 there are long lists of officials. There is careful attention to genealogy. I submit that Ezra as a teacher witnesses to Jews about *deep, shaping covenantal rootage,* about belonging to a community that lives in time for a long time, even through "the breach." Jews are not people adrift in the world; therefore, they cannot be detached or act in autonomous ways. The power of tradition (enacted in genealogy) is definitional. In liturgy and in economics, Jews must adhere to the enduring memory that gives assurance and holds expectations.

The Witness of the Wisdom Teachers

The second form of teaching that may be understood in light of the reality of exile and displacement is that of the wisdom teachers. Wisdom reflection and wisdom literature are no doubt very old in Israel, as elsewhere in the Middle East. It is a common view of scholars, nonetheless, that the collection of wisdom materials in such books as Proverbs, Job, and Ecclesiastes is a postexilic enterprise in Israel. It is the postexilic situation that made this intellectual activity important as well as necessary. The dating of wisdom materials is notoriously difficult, and we cannot be certain whether we are dealing with the date of the formulation of the material or the date of collection. In any case, here we are interested in what wisdom teaching must have intended in the postexilic period.

The wisdom materials are committed to the proposition that sense can be made out of daily experience by the slow, steady, patient discernment of patterns of behavior and experience that recur. Life is not a series of ad hoc happenings; it is the recurrence of patterns of hurt and healing that are ordered and guaranteed by God. One need not reinvent the wheel; one can learn by paying attention to the residue of experience that is available in the long-established and artistically rendered observations from the past.

This material, it is commonly judged, is peculiarly attractive in the postexilic period. First—and this is a negative reason—this material attracts because it does not depend on any of the constructs of Mosaic faith. It has no commitment to covenant, cult, or credo and scarcely speaks about God, God's action, or even God's demands. It finds such appeals intellectually embarrassing or, at the least, intellectually unnecessary. Such a posture was congruent with the judgment of some scholars that in the events of 587 Mosaic-covenantal tradition had indeed failed and was bankrupt. One of the intellectual options for Israel is to see whether, in light of 587, religious sense can be made of experience without appeal to these memories.

Second, positively, for the first time since David, Israel now has to live on someone else's turf and according to someone else's categories. From now on, Jews would find their home in Persian, Hellenistic, and Roman societies. The wisdom teachers are indeed transnational, transethnic teachers, for life is experienced in like manner among all peoples. The wisdom tradition from early on has been cosmopolitan and open to reflection from any quarter. Thus, in breaking loose from old theological convictions and in being open to non-Israelite experience, wisdom is peculiarly congenial to the postexilic situation.

But if this teaching seeks to stay free of the Israelite traditions, how can these teachers be said to be witnesses? To what do they witness, and how do they articulate that witness?

Following Klaus Koch[32] and Hans Heinrich Schmid,[33] many scholars suggest that the core intellectual construct of the wisdom teacher is a notion of "deed-consequence" (*Tat-*

Erfolge, Tun-Ergeben). That is, the wisdom teachers teach that the world of human experience and created order is a harmonized unity that has a nonnegotiable moral coherence to it that must be honored and can be ignored only at great cost. Thus, I shall argue, the wisdom teachers bore witness to the moral coherence of reality.

First, moral coherence is generated by God and is reflective of God's purpose and will. God is the guarantor of the process of deed and consequence. Second, the structure of deeds and consequences is, in the Book of Proverbs, named "righteousness" *(sedegah)*.[34] The world is ordered for righteousness, and human righteousness consists in doing deeds that yield positive results for the community. Third, the linkage of deeds and consequences is not hidden or inscrutable but can be detected by careful observation over a long period of time. Thus, concerning economics, the wisdom teachers observed that hard work brings prosperity, and indebtedness brings trouble. Concerning sexuality, the wisdom teachers learned that illicit relations are endlessly destructive. Concerning social relations, the wisdom teachers observed that fools and foolishness should be avoided because trouble comes with them.

This teaching is marvelously theological because it affirms that this linkage is the very structure of creation and reflects the will of the Creator. It is, at the same time, wondrously practical because it is rooted in and pertains to no grand theory but to the daily realities of decision making.[35] The wisdom teachers, by their specific and patient instruction, did indeed bear witness against the kind of careless, foolish notion that life has no ordered, enduring structure.

From this critical theological conviction we may derive three other matters.

1. While the wisdom teachers believe firmly in the pattern of deeds and consequences and believe that the pattern can be known, they are discerning enough to know and honest enough to acknowledge that life is filled with exceptions.

There are slippages to the connections. There are occasions when the deed does not produce the consequence, when the lazy prosper, when the careless succeed, when the foolish benefit. Conversely, there are times when the responsible suffer and fail. The wisdom teachers at their best are aware that human experience is too variegated to fit even into their own schemes and that slippages must be honored. That slippage may be taken seriously by (a) claiming that if we knew more we could find the pattern even in the apparent slippage, (b) acknowledging there is a deep irrational element in life that will not be tamed or explained, or (c) taking this unresolved issue as an arena for continuing reflection, which in part will yield to rational analysis and in part requires a theological posture that transcends ethical certitude.

Out of this awareness emerges the recognition that reflection on "deed and consequence" finally drives wisdom to the question of theodicy, the question of virtue in a world of irrationality. Wisdom thus may become a theodic settlement (as in Proverbs), or a theodic crisis (as in Job), or theodic indifference and agnosticism (as in Ecclesiastes). But however the issue be turned, by reflection on the relation of deed and consequence, the wisdom teachers must take the issue of the cosmic scope of justice as their focal question.

2. A second derivation from the notion of "deed and consequence" is the affirmation that life is a set of relationships, and the central human task is to determine how the parts are related to one another. These relationships, to be sure, are not hierarchical or even static. They are fluid, flexible, and on the move. But they are interrelated because life experience is not a series of discrete units. There is a coherence to all experience. Notice how this faith in creation fights against technical reason, which wants to bracket out all the important dimensions of ultimacy. The wisdom teachers are convinced that no part of human experience can be understood, utilized, or mastered unless it is seen as a part of the whole.

3. Another derivation, as von Rad has seen most clearly, is

that the wisdom teachers paid great attention to how they spoke about these connections.[36] The *how* of speech is crucial to the *what* of experience. If life is experienced as an unresolved tension between reasonable acts and inexplicable irrationality, between connection and slippage, our experience is a playful, experimental exploration in which we watch for more of the hidden pattern to be disclosed to us in particular experiences that are genuinely revelatory. This movement of disclosure and hiddenness does not happen in a single straight line, but each new disclosure opens some new hiddenness. To speak about, to teach, to bear witness to this strangeness requires language that is not flat and precise but is playful, open, teasing, and inviting—language that in its form and artfulness is congenial to the teasing way of our experience. It is clear that wisdom teachers are attentive to language because they must find ways of speaking that invite the learner into the field of knowing and not knowing, of waiting yet to discern.

Ongoing Moral Discourse

We finally arrive at our basic question about wisdom instruction. The teacher is a witness. This is a teaching enterprise quite in contrast to that of Ezra, for it is very short on tradition and rootage. Wisdom is often portrayed and caricatured as an indifferent, providential operation. I suggest, however, that the wisdom teachers bear relentless witness to this conviction: *To be human means to be endlessly involved in ethical reflection and moral discourse.* Such discourse is, of course, practical and rooted in experience. It does not, however, consist simply in ad hoc experience or in a narrow, prudential concern. Wisdom teaches that experience is large, wondrous, and intergenerational; what has been learned about the possibility of virtue and the consequence of action is pertinent and authoritative in every season of decision making.

The moral discourse sponsored here is an ongoing, unresolved conversation, because we always have again to probe our experience in relation to the larger residue of intergenerational wisdom observation. We are still and always will be at the edge of learning what to do and why we do it. This passion for continued moral discourse is a teaching against two temptations. On the one hand, wisdom instruction is against a kind of moral absolutism that imagines that there is a set of conclusions in the form of rules and pronouncements that only need to be reiterated because they are valid everywhere and always. Such an absolutism is rejected by the wisdom teachers because they know about slippage. There are always exceptions, and it takes hard, sustained reflection to see how the exceptions cohere with the pattern, if indeed they do.

On the other hand, passion for ongoing moral discourse is against a privatized moral indifference that believes that one act is as good as another, that a single person is a private agent whose actions do not make any difference, that in any event the universe is indifferent, and virtue or vice makes little difference beyond luck or crass utilitarianism.

Against the temptation, the wisdom teachers believe that issues of moral coherence place each moral agent in a network of moral agents, and what each does matters to all. The reason the wisdom teachers are inventively playful is that they believe the "deed-consequence" construct is utterly nonnegotiable and endlessly negotiable, and to fall out on either side is to misunderstand both our moral significance and our moral responsibility. The dialectic between negotiable and nonnegotiable means that the moral agent must be a skillful interpreter and a keen discerner to see in any particular circumstance what is given and what is chooseable. It is participation in this ongoing conversation that rescues us from the complacency of Proverbs and the cynicism of Ecclesiastes. The wisdom teachers believe that the very shape of cosmic reality is at work and at risk in our daily decision making. It really does matter how we live.

To be sure, this instruction lives at the far edge from the old covenantal instruction of Moses and the prophets. It is less inclined to the body of instruction in the Torah that Israel took as authoritative. It is more open to experience. There is a move in postexilic Judaism, however, culminating in Ben Sirach, arguing for the convergence and finally the identity of Israel's wisdom and Yahweh's Torah.[37] They are the same. The equation is already anticipated by the voice of Moses in Deut. 4:6:

> Keep [the commandments] and do them; for that will be your wisdom and your understanding in the sight of the peoples, who, when they hear all these statutes, will say, "Surely this great nation is a wise and understanding people."

Moses here anticipates that the nations will recognize that the Torah is indeed remarkable, wisdom judged by the sapiential norms of the people. Finally, Israel is drawn back to the Torah, back to Ezra, and ultimately back to Moses. But Israel is also able to linger with wisdom teachers and to do its reflection in the categories of other nations. Even on those grounds, Israel cannot avoid the moral dimension of reality. How human community lives is decisive for human destiny. We cannot hide in absolutes or escape into privatism. Everything is at issue in our capacity to discern and to act.

The Witness of the Apocalyptic

The third mode of instruction that emerges in the postexilic period is the apocalyptic. "Apocalyptic" refers to the disclosure of the future that is not derived from the present but is a new gift from and incursion by God that is beyond our categories of human life. Apocalyptic bears witness to the promised future and invites Israel to embrace its wondrous hope.

The future is no stranger in Israel. In the initial disclosure to Moses (Exod. 3:1–14), God had already said, "I will bring you to a good and broad land" (v. 8). The core conviction of Israel is that God will override the "here and now" with a new "then and there" that surpasses both our expectations and our discernment of how it could happen. While Israel celebrates the promised future, it never probes how that future is possible. Israel is content to believe that an inexplicable future is a function of the free sovereignty of Yahweh. Because Yahweh is a free sovereign, such an inexplicable future is a part of Israel's faith. Indeed, the Torah in its finished form is a tale of how God watches over the promise to give to Israel a future Israel could not secure for itself.[38]

But then came 587. It seemed that the power or will of God had failed. The present had run out, exhausted without a future. The old credo elements of the Exodus and the entry into the land no longer seemed pertinent. Israel was in a situation where it could well abandon all hope. It could settle for despair. And indeed that was one option. Ecclesiastes is a voice very close to despair, for the writer affirms that there is no new thing under the sun and what has been is what will be.

In the face of the despair to which Israel was tempted, there is another tradition that seizes the legacy of hope that is central to Yahwism. The motif of promise is present in the credo and surely in the great prophets. The matter, however, does not hinge on having a literary tradition to which appeal can be made. The real issue is not literary but theological. It concerns the character of God. The central conviction that concerns Israel in its failed tradition at the brink of despair is this: *The God of Israel has the capacity to work a public newness that is dreamed and thought and proposed only in the heart of God.*[39] That is indeed a mouthful, but it is the mouthful that sustained Israel in its despair. It is difficult to articulate the radicalness of the vocation of hope that lives in the face of conservative scribalism and that mocks liberal benignness, which does not really believe in a newness. This

tradition of prophetic-apocalyptic hope has a most robust view
of God and does not believe that God is contained in our
notions of the possible, or that God is simply a projection of
our best anticipations, or that "God has no hands but ours."

Apocalyptic builds on the prophetic promise. I cite one
such prophetic promise that characteristically asserts and neither argues nor demonstrates. Isaiah 11:1–9 is a well-known
promise of a coming king. The poem anticipates and celebrates a new human king.

> With righteousness he shall judge the poor,
>   and decide with equity for the meek of the earth. . . .
> Righteousness shall be the girdle of his waist,
>   and faithfulness the girdle of his loins.
>
> (Isa. 11:4–5)

That sounds like any political speech, and its implementation
is thinkable. But Israel's hope is characteristically restless
with such believable expectation. The promise pushes out
beyond the historically credible to the cosmically yearned for.

> The wolf shall dwell with the lamb,
>   and the leopard shall lie down with the kid. . . .
> The sucking child shall play over the hole of the asp,
>   and the weaned child shall put his hand on the adder's den.
> They shall not hurt or destroy in all my holy mountain.
>
> (Isa. 11:6–9)

The whole of creation will be made new and will at last
become the world God has intended. The whole of creation
will be mended. We are not told how or when. We are told
only why—because Yahweh has decreed it. As a result of that
decree, the present animosity of wolf and lamb is no longer
absolute. We need not honor that arrangement so seriously
because it will not last.

This hope of a cosmic possibility is seized upon in the later
Isaiah tradition. Isaiah 65:17–25 dares to hope in a larger
scope. Now there is an anticipation of a new heaven and a new
earth, a new Jerusalem that is here characterized in detail. It

will be an arena of joy in which there will be no more weeping for brutality, no more distress in disadvantage (v. 19). There will be no more infant mortality (v. 20), no more rapacious economic policy that denies persons their rightful produce (vv. 21–22). As in Isa. 11, v. 25 anticipates full restoration of creation. Wolf and lamb feed together and none shall hurt anyone. The poetry powerfully contrasts the way things are with how they will be. The power of the rhetoric is to let the vision for a moment override the shabbiness of the present. This kind of voice is not embarrassed by the unexplained gap between this age and the age to come. It is content to let the gap stand, convinced that the substance of new possibility more than compensates for our inability to say how.

If we ask who could speak this way or why would anyone speak this way, we answer, people like Martin Luther King, Jr., who have a dream.[40] King did not have a concrete sense about how to get from here to there. But the purpose of his dream, like Isa. 65:17–25, is to rescue caring people from their despair and to move them to action. The purpose of the dream is to show that the present sorriness is not eternal but will end and be displaced by the new intentionality of God.

In Isa. 65:17–25, however, we are not quite yet at apocalyptic. Apocalyptic teaching is visioning, hoping, and expecting where the present has failed to provide any ground for hope. There is a realism about the Old Testament that finds apocalyptic embarrassing and dangerous. Even so, however, the apocalyptic element has happily not been fully screened out. The Book of Daniel, at the edge of the canon, gives us tales of hope in daring language.

Daniel 4 is a tale about Nebuchadnezzar, remembered king of Babylon, tyrant par excellence, here a paradigm for worldly power that resists the purpose of God.[41] Jews found it possible to lay upon this model figure all their resentment and hostility about the present unjust age. Nebuchadnezzar, we are told, had his life all worked out, as the rulers of this age do. As long as he kept control, he was unbothered.

But God uses dreams as the "royal road" to an alternative (Dan. 4:5). The king could not manage his dreams. The God of the future still governs dreams, even those of Nebuchadnezzar. The dream disturbed the king because it asserted that the future of Nebuchadnezzar was not as secure as he had imagined. The Babylonian wise men and technologists could not handle tho dream because it had come from another source. They were skilled in arms and finance but not at dreams which ran outside their technical purview (vv. 6–7).

But there is Daniel, a faithful Jew who knows and can interpret what all the empire of Babylon cannot handle (vv. 8–9). The faithful have peculiar access to God's future. After the summary of the dream in vv. 10–18, Daniel interprets. The dream is of a great tree to be hewed down. The tree, says Daniel, "is you, O king" (v. 22). It is Nebuchadnezzar and Babylon and all the great powers of this age which are to be cut down. This arrogant, seemingly unchallengeable king shall be

> driven from among men, and your dwelling shall be with the beasts of the field; you shall be made to eat grass like an ox, and you shall be wet with the dew of heaven, and seven times shall pass over you, till you know that the Most High rules the kingdom of men, and gives it to whom he will (Dan. 4:25).

The intent of the dream and of the "cutting down" is that Nebuchadnezzar shall recognize the rule of Yahweh. It did not take long for the dream to become, in the context of the narrative, a reality.

> Immediately the word was fulfilled upon Nebuchadnezzar. He was driven from among men, and ate grass like an ox, and his body was wet with the dew of heaven (v. 33).

All the rulers of this age are reduced to impotence, humiliation, and disgust. In the end, Nebuchadnezzar prays to the Most High (vv. 34–35) and receives his throne back (vv. 36–37). The restoration is from Yahweh. The throne is restored only because the king has become appropriately submissive to Yahweh.

This sort of tale and this sort of faith are enormously problematic for us. It has long been an embarrassment to mainline religion and has been pushed to the very edge of our theological awareness. It is so radical as to be outrageous. We need, however, to ask if the problem is with the faith claim of the literature or with our posture of resistance to that claim.

The theological substance of this trajectory is to assert that the present is not absolute or eternal and cannot be ultimately sustained. Moreover, God's future is not an extrapolation from the present but is given in a sovereign act of discontinuity. It is plausible that this material is treasured among the world-weary, who can no longer expect anything from this age. The turn toward a new age can, of course, be an escapism, but it may also be a bold rejection of despair. Those who despair believe that how things now are is how they will always be. If we believe that long enough, we will conform and have the horizon of our imagination severely tailored to fit the present.

The teacher who witnesses in this literature makes a different case. This teaching is an insistence that reality should not be perceived in the domesticated categories of the immediate present. No present arrangement should set the limit to our hope or fear or desire. No present arrangement is permitted to crush our spirit, because the God who summons us is not a party to that present arrangement.

This teacher thus means to instruct the people in a *radical subversive hope* that delegitimates, destabilizes, and deconstructs all the best present commitments for the sake of another possibility.[42]

It is now argued by a number of scholars that the extreme limit of apocalyptic hope is found in resurrection faith, in the conviction that God has the power and the will to work life out of death. There is no doubt that resurrection belongs in the linguistic, imaging circle of apocalyptic. Most of the "enlightened" talk about resurrection and especially the resurrection of Jesus has torn that affirmation out of its apocalyptic context. Then Jesus' resurrection is at most an oddity that needs to be explained away on alien grounds. But when the event of resurrection is restored in its proper context, we are faced with the foundational question of whether the power of death will have the last say. We discern the power of death in Israel's exile, in Jesus' Friday, in Beirut's brutality, in Johannesburg's inhumanity, in Liverpool's unemployment, in drugged teenagers, in despairing affluence, in bad marriages, in the face of nuclear annihilation. We do not need to look long or hard to see the rampant power of death among us. When our faith is contained in those categories, we are unable to act. The permit to act comes only in the conviction that God's power for life can override and outdistance death. This teacher witnesses to subversiveness by a strange story. The story is so strange because we would rather explain it away than meet its claim. But if we explain it away, we explain away our own possible future. We are, willy-nilly, children of that odd future.

The Importance of Scribalism, Wisdom, and Apocalyptic

These three teachers—Ezra the scribe, who witnesses to *shaping rootage;* the wisdom teacher, who witnesses to *ongoing ethical conversation;* and the apocalyptic teacher, who witnesses to *subversive visions of possibility*—all draw upon and are derived from the Mosaic source. All are, at the same time, new models, responding to the new postexilic situation in which the old Mosaic-Levitic-prophetic model was not fully adequate.

One can sense the power and significance of these teaching efforts if one considers the condition of faith where these teachers do not witness. Thus, without the scribe the community would be adrift without *a shaping past.* Without the wisdom teacher the community would be indifferent to and unaware of the cruciality of *present moral discourse* as a way to be human together. Without the apocalyptic witness the community would be submerged in the present without a summons to *an alternative future*. The teaching witness keeps alive an alternative sense of past, present, and future and so echoes the intent of Moses.

Finally, I need to say something about how I have framed this argument. It might have been expected that I should make a more "contemporary" argument, less biblically shaped, more directly dealing with contemporary problematics in a pluralistic, "value-free" educational setting. I have chosen this way for two reasons. First, I do not believe we can speak in empty, formal categories about teaching as witness without considering specific teaching that makes a concrete substantive witness. And if one is to take up a substantive witness, then the models that emerge from the Bible are as legitimate as any other.

Second, I believe that the particular substance I have outlined from the Old Testament is in some form urgent in our culture. I do not review the material of the Old Testament simply as generally illustrative, but because I believe that these claims for *the past as shaping rootage, the present as an arena for moral discourse*, and *the future as subversive vision* are urgent in present-day culture. I do not imagine that these models can be taken over wholesale, but we shall have to see how these same insistences are appropriately presented for our season.

Let me say why I think that this offer of scribalism, wisdom, and apocalyptic is appropriate and urgent for us. Everything depends on how we read our context. Robert Bellah and his associates in *Habits of the Heart* have shown how an uncritical individualism is now the dominant mode of experience and perception in the West.[43] The individual is the unit of meaning and significance, and life is confined to quite private meanings and satisfactions that screen out all larger communal values and issues. Bellah's analysis has for me been underscored and supported by two earlier studies.

In 1962 Crawford McPherson published *The Political Theory of Possessive Individualism*,[44] a study of Hobbes and Locke that greatly illuminates our present economic situation and therefore our scheme of social values and practices. Hobbes (who lies behind Adam Smith and, in subsequent form, the entire Reagan-Yuppie revolution of greed) opined that each person is at war with every other. Locke, in his urbane passion for freedom, argued in an "enlightened" way that each has the freedom (and therefore the right) to seize as much of life as is available. The implication of Locke's argument is that personhood consists in acquiring and possessing, even if that means the possession of other persons for the sake of one's own well-being. This individualism is acquisitive drive.

In 1984 Alasdair MacIntyre published *After Virtue*, a study of the loss of common shared values and the coming of what he calls "emotive individualism."[45] By "emotive individualism" he means that the individual person is the final arbiter of value and that individual judgment is rooted in private need and desire. The result is that any public discourse about shared values, shared norms, or shared witness is an impossibility.

Bellah's analysis of individualism is a sociological study. But it is strongly supported by the economic analysis of McPherson and the critical philosophical reflection of MacIntyre. The individualism of Bellah is precisely *possessive* and *emotive*, that is, devoted to controlling and subject to no norm outside itself.

I submit that such individualism, possessive and emotive, is the context of any serious teaching in present-day Western culture. Given such individualism, which is pathological and destructive, teaching as witness is an odd notion, for it suggests inviting the learner and the learning community to share in and reflect upon a particular alternative claim, to make a commitment out beyond one's self, needs, and desires to a larger public, social possibility.

Our Enlightenment and post-Enlightenment situation does not in any particular or simple way parallel the Judean postexilic context. I do propose, however, that the urgings made by teachers in that cultural context are pertinent for us today. Our key pastoral, educational issue is to consider an alternative to the emotive, possessive individualism out of which a viable human community cannot be formed and in which serious public discourse is not possible. Teachers are not mandated to witness against individualism. Far better, more urgent, and more important is the intentional act of including learners in a shaping rootage, an ongoing conversation, and a subversive vision. In such a way, individualism may be placed in context and perchance redeemed. The absence of a serious past, a critiqued present, and a dangerous future inevitably leaves us with a greedy, anxious "now," expressed as either raw brutality or numbing despair. Moses had imagined an alternative. We could be apprentice teachers to Moses.

Notes

1. On the elusiveness of the evidence and the difficulty of drawing conclusions, see James L. Crenshaw, "Education in Ancient Israel," *Journal of Biblical Literature* 104 (1985): 601–15.
2. Of all the Old Testament materials, it may be least persuasive to suggest that the wisdom materials offer a convinced, passionate, partisan perspective. However, I believe a case can be made even here that this is not a neutral instructional enterprise, but fosters a quite intentional perspective in which a great deal is at stake. Here I identify that sapiential perspective as an insistence on an ongoing ethical conversation.
3. See James A. Sanders, "Adaptable for Life: The Nature and Function of Canon," in *Magnalia Dei: The Mighty Acts of God*, ed. Frank Moore Cross, Werner E. Lemke, and Patrick D. Miller, Jr. (New York: Doubleday & Co., 1976), 532–60. Sanders nicely refers to this as a "monotheizing" tendency, which is not hardened monotheism but which makes a truth claim which tends to exclude other truth claims.

60   WALTER BRUEGGEMANN

4. Gerhard von Rad, *The Problem of the Hexateuch and Other Essays* (New York: McGraw-Hill, 1966), 3–8.
5. Norman K. Gottwald, *The Tribes of Yahweh* (Maryknoll, N.Y.: Orbis Books, 1979), 72–114.
6. On the dramatic sequence of hurt, criticism, and imagination, see Walter Brueggemann, *Hope Within History* (Atlanta: John Knox Press, 1986), 7–26. More generally on Mosaic leadership, see Aaron Wildavsky, *The Nursing Father: Moses as a Political Leader* (Tuscaloosa: University of Alabama Press, 1984).
7. On the Sinai meeting as a decision about political sovereignty, see Martin Buber, *Kingship of God* (London: George Allen & Unwin, 1967). On the political implications of that covenantal decision, see George E. Mendenhall, "The Conflict Between Value Systems and Social Control," in *Unity and Diversity: Essays in the History, Literature, and Religion of the Ancient Near East*, ed. Hans Goedicke and J. J. M. Roberts (Baltimore: Johns Hopkins University Press, 1975), 169–80.
8. On the core witness, see Walter Harrelson, "Life, Faith, and the Emergence of Tradition," in *Tradition and Theology in the Old Testament*, ed. Douglas A. Knight (Philadelphia: Fortress Press, 1977), 11–30.
9. Von Rad, *The Problem of the Hexateuch and Other Essays*, 48–78; and idem, *Old Testament Theology* (Edinburgh: Oliver & Boyd, 1962), 1:129–305.
10. Gottwald, in *The Tribes of Yahweh*, makes as one of his major premises the notion that the Exodus material is not a historical report but a residue of ongoing sociological praxis. From a very different perspective, see the same point by Michael Walzer, *Exodus and Revolution* (New York: Basic Books, 1985).
11. The phrase is from Karl Barth, *The Word of God and the Word of Man* (London: Hodder & Stoughton, 1928). Barth grasped most clearly the epistemological oddness of the Bible. The teacher as witness must struggle precisely with that epistemological oddness.
12. On education as induction into membership, see the shrewd analysis by Thomas F. Green, "Walls," an informal unpublished seminar paper prepared for the Center for Congregational Life, National Faculty Seminar. For a shrewd and subtle account of an alternative "membership," see Wendell Berry, *The Wild*

Birds (San Francisco: North Point Press, 1986).

13. See Walter Brueggemann, *The Creative Word* (Philadelphia: Fortress Press, 1982), 14–39; and J. Alberto Soggin, "Cultic-Aetiological Legends and Catechesis in the Hexateuch," *Old Testament and Oriental Studies*, Biblica et Orientalea 29 (Rome: Biblical Institute Press, 1975): 72–77.

14. Gerhard E. Lenski, *Power and Privilege: A Theory of Social Stratification* (New York: McGraw-Hill, 1966) has been an important reference for Gottwald's attention to stratification and egalitarianism in ancient Israel. The question of justice concerns precisely the problem of stratification, which the revolution of Moses resisted.

15. The decisive study of this poem is George Ernest Wright's "The Law-Suit of God: A Form-Critical Study of Deuteronomy 32," in *Israel's Prophetic Heritage*, ed. Bernhard W. Anderson and Walter Harrelson (London: SCM Press, 1962): 26–67.

16. Wright, "The Law-Suit of God," 54–58.

17. On this contradiction, see Walter Brueggemann, "A Shape for Old Testament Theology, I: Structure Legitimation," *Catholic Biblical Quarterly* 47 (1985):28–46, and "A Shape for Old Testament Theology. II: Embrace of Pain," *Catholic Biblical Quarterly* 47 (1985): 395–415.

18. On Joshua as the installed successor to Moses, see Dennis J. McCarthy, "An Installation Genre?" *Journal of Biblical Literature* 90 (1971): 31–41.

19. On the commonality of these texts, see James Muilenburg, "The Form and Structure of the Covenantal Formulations," *Vetus Testamentum* 9 (1959): 347–65.

20. Gerhard von Rad, *Studies in Deuteronomy* (London: SCM Press, 1953), 60–69. See the critical assessment of Ernest W. Nicholson, *Deuteronomy and Tradition* (Oxford: Basil Blackwell & Mott, 1967), 58–82. On Levitical preaching in the Books of Chronicles (perhaps derivative from that of Deuteronomy), see von Rad, *The Problem of the Hexateuch and Other Essays*, 267–80; and Jacob Meyers, "The Kerygma of the Chronicler," *Interpretation* 20 (1966): 259–73.

21. Hans Walter Wolff, "Hoseas geistige Heimat," *Theologische Literaturzeitung* 81 (1956): 83–94.

22. Gottwald, *The Tribes of Yahweh*, 489–97.

23. On the lawsuit speech in the prophets, see Claus Westermann, *Basic Forms of Prophetic Speech* (London: Lutterworth Press, 1967). On the prophetic use of older Mosaic memories for purposes of criticism and interpretation, see Michael Walzer, *Interpretation and Social Criticism* (Cambridge: Harvard University Press, 1987), 67–94.

24. On these voices of exile, see Walter Brueggemann, *Hopeful Imagination* (Philadelphia: Fortress Press, 1986), and von Rad, *Old Testament Theology* (Edinburgh: Oliver & Boyd, 1965), 2:263–77.

25. On teachers as interpreters, see James L. Kugel and Rowan Greer, *Early Biblical Interpretation* (Philadelphia: Westminster Press, 1986), 52–72. I have found Kugel especially helpful for the preparation of this paper.

26. Jacob Neusner, *Understanding Seeking Faith* (Atlanta: Scholars Press, 1986), 115–49.

27. See Brueggemann, *Hopeful Imagination.* It is clear that the discernment of exile and restoration as presented by Jeremiah, Ezekiel, and 2 Isaiah was not a simple report on facts but an enormously bold, poetic construal which fought against other construals which also had compelling adherents.

28. Neusner, *Understanding Seeking Faith,* 145.

29. On the theological crisis and pluralism in emerging Judaism, see Michael E. Stone, *Sects and Visions: A Profile of Judaism from Ezra to the Jewish Revolts* (Philadelphia: Fortress Press, 1980); and John J. Collins, *Between Athens and Jerusalem: Jewish Identity in the Hellenistic Diaspora* (New York: Crossroad, 1983).

30. See H. G. M. Williamson, *Ezra, Nehemiah* (Waco: Word, 1985); and idem, *Ezra and Nehemiah* (Sheffield, Eng.: JSOT Press, 1987).

31. Kugel, I suggest, is committed to the notion that it is the very act of interpretation that is constitutive for Judaism. Kugel, *Early Biblical Interpretation,* 38, concludes, "It was precisely the intermittent obsession with past events and the necessity of having them bear on the present that gave interpretation of all kinds its urgency." In addition to "obsession with past events," I should say it was also obsession with past *texts.*

32. Klaus Koch, "Is There a Doctrine of Retribution in the Old

Testament?" in *Theodicy in the Old Testament*, ed. James L. Crenshaw (Philadelphia: Fortress Press, 1983), 57–87.

33. Hans Heinrich Schmid, *Wesen und Geschichte der Weisheit* (Berlin: Topelmann, 1966).

34. See especially Hans Heinrich Schmid, *Gerechtigkeit als Weltordnung* (Tübingen: J. C. B. Mohr [Siebeck], 1968). Schmid has made the most formidable case that "righteousness" is not a set of moral acts or delivering acts but is an element in the very structure of creation as ordained by God.

35. See Gerhard von Rad, *Wisdom in Israel* (Nashville: Abingdon Press, 1972), 57–73. Von Rad (p. 62) speaks of the convergence of an "experience of God" and an "experience of the world."

36. Von Rad, *Wisdom in Israel*, 24–50, has most fully explored the artistic dimension of proverbial wisdom as a particularly skillful way of rendering experienced reality. On the power and intention of such speech, see also James L. Crenshaw, "Wisdom and Authority: Sapiential Rhetoric and Its Warrants," Supplement to *Vetus Testamentum* 32 (1981): 10–29. On the inextricable relation of the "How" of speech and the "What" of faith, see esp. Gail R. O'Day, *Revelation in the Fourth Gospel: Narrative Mode and Theological Claim* (Philadephia: Fortress Press, 1986).

37. See Gerald T. Sheppard, *Wisdom as a Hermeneutical Construct* (Berlin: Walter de Gruyter, 1980) for one important exploration of the ways in which sapiential influences have decisively shaped the canon.

38. See David J. A. Clines, *The Theme of the Pentateuch* (Sheffield, Eng.: Dept. of Biblical Studies, 1978) for the cruciality of promise for the totality of the Pentateuch.

39. Donald Gowan, *Eschatology in the Old Testament* (Philadelphia: Fortress Press, 1985) has provided a convenient and suggestive summary of the theological motif of hope in the Old Testament.

40. On hope as a crucial factor for "history-makers," see Brueggemann, *Hope Within History*, 49–71.

41. For a most remarkable and suggestive theological interpretation of the Daniel materials, see John Goldingay, "The Stories of Daniel: A Narrative Politics," *Journal for the Study of the Old Testament* 37 (1987): 99–116.

64   WALTER BRUEGGEMANN

42. The language and function of this tradition is not unlike "Utopia," as it is characterized by Paul Ricoeur, *Lectures on Ideology and Utopia* (New York: Columbia University Press, 1986), 173, 179, 182, and passim.
43. Robert H. Bellah et al., *Habits of the Heart: Individualism and Commitment in American Life* (Berkeley and Los Angeles: University of California Press, 1985).
44. Crawford McPherson, *The Political Theory of Possessive Individualism: Hobbes to Locke* (Oxford: Clarendon Press, 1962).
45. Alasdair MacIntyre, *After Virtue: A Study in Moral Theory* (Notre Dame, Ind.: University of Notre Dame Press, 1984).

CHAPTER 3

Transmitting the Jewish Heritage from Generation to Generation

Samuel E. Karff

A NUMBER OF YEARS AGO THIS STORY WAS MAKING THE rounds of the American Jewish community:

Sadie asked her travel agent to arrange a trip to a remote village in the Himalayas, where she was planning to visit a certain guru. The trip was arranged, and after several days of strenuous travel by air and pack animal, Sadie arrived at her destination.

Hearing her request for an immediate meeting with the guru, the village greeter first informed Sadie that no audiences were being granted that week. When Sadie persisted, the greeter relented: "All right, you may see his holiness, but you may speak to him only three words. Is that agreeable?" Sadie accepted the condition. She entered the large hall, stood before the guru, and plaintively exclaimed, "Sheldon, come home."

At the time of its circulation, this story stirred both laughter and sighs of poignant recognition. Sadie, the Jewish mother, was pleading for her son to return to his patrimony, his own sacred space. Sheldon's apparent defection from Judaism violated his obligation to keep the covenant and her obligation to transmit it.

The classic Jewish soul is gripped by a passion to transmit the heritage from generation to generation. A rabbinic commentary to a primary Jewish prayer underscores the point. When in prayer the congregation recites "Hear O Israel, the Lord is our God, the Lord is One," it is customary to follow that proclamation with the words "Praised be His name whose glorious kingdom is forever and ever."

What, asked the rabbis, is the origin of this dual prayer? They answer: When Jacob (his name having since been changed to Israel) lay on his deathbed, he summoned his twelve children and said: "My grandfather Abraham inaugurated the covenant. He passed it on to Isaac, my father, who passed it on to me. Now I wonder what will happen after I am gone. Will you keep the faith?" The children replied: "Hear O Israel, our Father, the Lord is our God, the Lord is One." Whereupon before closing his eyes Jacob-Israel responded: "If you will bear witness to the faith, then praised be His name whose glorious kingdom is forever and ever."[1]

Central to Judaism is this passion to pass the Torah from generation to generation. Our daily prayers include the biblical injunction "You shall teach them diligently to your children" (Deut. 6:7).

In a remarkable lecture to the Jewish community of Frankfurt in 1934, Martin Buber expressed the eternal resonance of the covenant: "The life of the spirit of the people is renewed whenever a teaching generation transmits it to a learning generation which in turn, growing into teachers, transmits the spirit through the lips of new teachers to the ears of new pupils."[2]

The Parent as Teacher

The primary teacher is the parent. That responsibility is reflected in Jewish literature through the ages. In fifteenth-century Toledo, Rabbi Israel Ibn Al Nakawa wrote a popular manual for Jewish living. One section, titled "Concerning the Rearing of Children," describes the father's role as religious model.

> When father gets up early to pray he should take his child with him to the synagogue; and when he is enroute to perform an act of lovingkindness (such as visiting the sick, arranging a dowry for a poor bride, or accompanying the dead to their last resting place, and the like) so he will accustom his son to acts of lovingkindness and the performance of the commandments.[3]

Al Nakawa's treatise also mandates the father to involve his son in the building of the Sukkah, the fruit-adorned booth, which marks the observance of the Feast of Tabernacles (Booths).

Note that this medieval manual for Jewish living is very male centered, a given from ancient times to the present day. To be sure, mothers in the Hebrew Bible play crucial roles in the transmission of the covenant. Rebecca, for instance, saw to it that Jacob was chosen over Esau.

An ancient sage, Rabbi Tahlifa of Caesarea, acknowledged the importance of the maternal role. He taught that at God's command Moses expounded the details of the covenant to the women first. God reasoned:

> When I created the world I only commanded Adam first and then Eve was commanded through Adam with the result that she transgressed and upset the world. If I don't now call women first they will nullify the Torah. For this reason does it say "thus shalt thou say to the *house* of Jacob [i.e., women of the house]."[4]

The classic tradition, exceptions aside, is decidedly male oriented. The father, not the mother, has the responsibility of instructing his son in his religious duties. Girls were taught by their mothers how to be faithful daughters of the covenant, to bake the *challah*, to observe the special rules of ritual purity, including immersion in the ritual bath, and to light the Sabbath candles. Mothers in Israel received special merit by seeing to it that their children received an education, but this task was specifically the mandate of the father.

Formal instructors in the tradition outside the home also were males. The synagogue and the community school were primarily male domains through the Middle Ages and until modern times. Obviously, the male centeredness of religious education has been challenged and changed, especially by non-Orthodox segments of the contemporary Jewish community.

Haggadah and Halakah

Al Nakawa's medieval manual included two kinds of classic religious education. The first, the Haggadah, contains the stories of the faith. These stories mediated a basic understanding of God's relation to the world and the Jewish people. The Haggadah includes the story of God's creation of the world, the deliverance of Israel from Egyptian bondage, and the giving of the tablets on Mount Sinai, as well as rabbinic stories elaborating upon these biblical themes. By telling these narratives, adults conveyed to children the sense of a God who created and sustained the world, who is redemptively involved in that world—my world—and who teaches me the way I should live if I am to fulfill my role in God's world.

The second kind of teaching, the Halakah, is the exposition of the way Jews are commanded to live as sons or daughters of the covenant. Whereas the Haggadah embodies an understanding of religious truth (i.e., how and why things are in God's world), the Halakah commands not what I must believe but how I must act. Belief is mediated through the stories of the Haggadah. One's actions are structured by the commandments embodied in the Halakah. Those obligations are based on citable biblical texts or creative rabbinic interpretation of biblical texts.

It is important to note that one of the fundamental deeds

imposed upon a Jew is to study the Torah. The purpose of study, however, is not to acquire wisdom or an understanding of God's relationship to the world. Study is of value only if it leads to living the covenant, that is, fulfilling the commandments. In the earlier-mentioned lecture to the Jewish community, Martin Buber declared:

> Among all the people in the world Israel is probably the only one in which wisdom that does not lead directly to the unity of knowledge and deed is meaningless. . . . The simple man who acts is given precedence over the scholar whose knowledge is not expressed in deeds.[5]

Study and Action

Study is important because it leads to action. Study is also important because it provides guidance and a ground for right action. In the morning liturgy, Jews thank God for teaching our ancestors and us "the laws of life." "Incline our hearts to know and understand, to hear, learn, teach, observe, do and sustain all the words of Your Torah with love." Buber adds: "The teaching cannot be severed from the deed, neither can the deed be severed from the teachings."[6]

The ancient Jew studied in order to discover "the laws of life." The modern Jew, attuned to the American zeitgeist, has lost that sense of searching in one's heritage for the way to live. No one has more poignantly described the contemporary mind-set than Allan Bloom. He writes of bright university students who engage in "value clarification," a pooling of their deeply felt attitudes toward life. For the most part they have lost the sense of a nourishing heritage. They may not really believe that one way of responding to life is compellingly truer or nobler. One simply probes feelings and chooses a life style, and one life style is as intrinsically justifiable as another.

Such "value clarification" exercises are impoverished by a lack of rootedness in time-hallowed texts. While today's students believe it to be a great virtue to get in touch with their feelings (and to respect the feelings of others), they have lost the sense of a life grounded in values beyond simple subjectivity or prudentialism. Bloom laments the bright, decent students who can say nothing more profound about the ground of their moral action than, "If I did it to him, he could do it to me."7

Religious education faithful to the covenant perspective seeks to implant the sense that "A good teaching has been given to you, do not forsake My Torah" (Prov. 4:2). The primary purpose of religious education is to furnish the mind with guides for conduct that fulfill the intended purpose of our lives. If we succeed, then a Jew contemplating whether or not to abort a fetus, or a couple considering in vitro fertilization, or Jews deciding whether to work on Yom Kippur will feel the need to respond with an informed heart. They will be moved to ask, What ought I do in this situation if I am to fulfill my covenant as a son/daughter of Israel?

The liberal Jewish educator acknowledges the need to negate certain mandates from the past. But authenticity requires that even our negations be grounded in the heritage. Thus we may feel compelled to reject much of traditional Judaism's male domination, but we do so in the name of a fundamental principle embodied in Torah: Man *and* woman are created in the image of God. That which denies either dignity demeans the Creator.

Study is important because it informs action. Action, doing the deed, is important because it may best lead to trust and belief. In this connection we should also note that, from childhood on, the home, synagogue, and Jewish school did not and do not make acceptance of a carefully structured set of beliefs the litmus test of fidelity to the covenant. Belief was articulated basically and effectively through the Haggadah, the great stories about God's relationship to Israel and the world. Jewish educators (priests, teachers, rabbis) focused more on limiting the parameters of acceptable conduct than belief.

That, says one rabbi, was the teaching strategy of the Supreme Educator. The rabbis imagined God saying: "Would that My people forsook Me but observed My commandments, for by observing My commandments they will come to know Me."[8] God reasons that by living within the covenant, by observing the responsibilities of the covenant, one will come to appreciate and affirm the God of the covenant.

To this day Jews do not exact from either a potential member of a congregation, a convert, or a confirmand, a clearly delineated understanding of the way God works in the world. Instead, Jews seek a commitment to live within the covenant, to observe its teachings and transmit them to the next generation.

The most difficult challenge for the non-Orthodox Jewish educator is to walk the narrow ridge between the past and the present. As Jews we cannot accept all the established mandates of the past as the will of God for us, but we still seek to ground our life and our people's in the commanding voice that speaks through the teachings of the Torah.

The Primary Years

Judaism places great emphasis on the learning that occurs in the primary years. The Talmud enjoins that if a child is able to speak, his father must teach him the Torah and the recitation of the Shema: "Hear O Israel, the Lord is our God, the Lord is One." What can a young child, an infant, learn of the Torah? A child can learn the simple verse "Moses commanded us the Torah, it belongs to the congregation of Jacob" (Deut. 33:4).[9]

The sages also reason that in temple times, if a child was old enough to eat roast meat—even a piece no larger than the size of an olive—the paschal lamb could be slaughtered in that child's behalf. In a similar vein, although a child is not obligated to hear the sound of the shofar on Rosh Hashanah, still he is to be taught, as a child, how it is sounded. If he should experiment by sounding the shofar even on the Sabbath, when such sounding is normally prohibited to adults, the child should not be stopped.[10] While a child was not expected to fast on Yom Kippur until the age of thirteen, a parent should instruct him well before his thirteenth birthday that he is permitted to fast part of the day.[11]

Undoubtedly, the classic primary learning situation for a child was the Passover meal, the Seder supper. The Bible commands the Israelite annually to tell of God's mighty acts and celebrate Israel's deliverance from Egyptian bondage. Apart from the instruction to eat unleavened bread and (in temple times) sacrifice a paschal lamb, the principal instruction is to "tell the story to your children" (Exod. 13:8).

To tell the story, the ancient rabbis developed the ritual of the Seder supper, a structured meal in which the story is told while the family is sitting around the table. Edible props (matzo, bitter herbs, and so forth) lend pungent vividness to the story.

But how can one be certain that the story reaches the child? First, by telling the child that a piece of matzo (the *Afikomen*) will be hidden. That piece of matzo is to be broken up and distributed to those seated around the table at the conclusion of the meal. The child is told that at the appropriate time (if he or she stays awake along enough) the one who finds the *Afikomen* may insist that it be redeemed for a price. This incentive, plus a vividly illustrated liturgy telling the story of Pharaoh's wickedness (the ten plagues) and the miracle of deliverance, is calculated to catch the attention of the children.

Even more central is the role children play in telling the story. The liturgy (called the Haggadah, i.e., "telling the story") contains four questions, which the youngest verbal child is trained to ask. The first question is: "Wherefore is this night different from all other nights? On other nights we eat leavened and unleavened bread, on this night only unleavened bread?" The child asks four such questions and the parent responds. Thus the child is ritually involved in the telling of the tale.

Perhaps most critical of all is that portion of the Passover liturgy that speaks of four kinds of children: the wise (intellectual) one wants a full, nuanced description of the festival; the simple child wants a direct explanation, a bottom-line report; the wicked child insists this event has nothing to do with him or her; a fourth child is so uninstructed he or she does not even know what question to ask. It is important, then, that the message of Passover be conveyed to all in a manner congruent with their needs and sensibilities. None is expendable. All are to be reached if the commandment "You shall tell your child" is to be fulfilled.[12]

Formal Schooling

While parents were considered the primary religious educators, even in talmudic times considerable emphasis was placed on formal schooling. Before the modern era, religious education took precedence over what today is called secular education. The latter was often subsumed or appended to the former—or neglected altogether.

In America today most Jewish children spend the greatest portion of their formal learning hours in a secular school. Supplementary religious education is provided in a two-days-a-week, late afternoon "Hebrew school" and/or a weekend morning "religious school." This model has been especially favored by the Reform movement, which has championed the cause of Jewish integration into the mainstream of American life. The cost of this model has been considerable.

This model signals to the child that secular education is primary. Religious education is secondary. One's best learning hours are devoted to math and social studies, not Hebrew or Torah. Moreover, how does one begin to do justice to a millennial heritage in a few-hours-a-week program that takes an often reluctant child away from afternoon play time or weekend recreational options? No less sobering is the absence of any symbolic reinforcement of a religious life perspective during the many hours spent in the secular school. Most Jews prefer the price of church-state separation to a school system directly or subtly reinforcing the religious symbols of the Christian majority.

But this dramatic attenuation of formal religious instruction in modern times is accompanied by a strong diminution in the religious literacy of parents and in their inclination or capacity to be effective religious models. This is especially problematical for a tradition that so heavily accents home observance.

How should liberal Jews cope with the problem? It is not easy. Apart from parenting centers and the greatly expanded Jewish summer camp program movement, the most radical response by the Reform movement has been the endorsement of Jewish day schools. In the past such schools were the exclusive domain of more traditional Jews. We liberals regarded them as self-segregating threats to our integration. As a Reform rabbi, I shared that position until quite recently.

I am now persuaded that if liberal Judaism is to be spared from shallowness, we ought to provide a day school track, at least in the primary grades. Such an option enables children to experience Jewish religious education as an integral part of their human self-discovery. When science is taught, we can expect teachers to convey that science asks and answers important questions, but also that there are other even more important questions that science cannot answer. Such a setting provides ample opportunity for prayer as an integral part of daily life. The Jewish day school student has multiple occasions to feel included in the larger American society. Such a child is perhaps even better prepared to enter and live in that society as an informed, self-respecting Jew.

Bar Mitzvah and Bat Mitzvah

One of the most significant milestones in the life of a family is the Bar/Bat Mitzvah ceremony. The child usually prepares by attending weekday afternoon Hebrew school in addition to Sabbath school. Here he or she learns to read Hebrew scripture from the Torah scroll as well as the Hebrew prayers and the Sabbath liturgy.

At thirteen a boy, and at twelve a girl, is presumed to have reached the age of religious responsibility. The term *Bar Mitzvah* signifies a son of the Jewish deed; *Bat Mitzvah*, a daughter of the Jewish deed. The child is now accountable for religious deeds that heretofore were the privilege and burden of the parents. Before reaching the age of religious maturity, the child sees the parents fast on Yom Kippur but is told he or she is not required to do so. The daughter watches the mother light and bless the Sabbath candles but may not do so herself. The son watches the father constitute one of the ten males required for a public worship service or sees his father called up to bless the Torah but is not himself eligible to do so. At Bar or Bat Mitzvah the child becomes accountable for these acts.

In our congregation, when the Bar/Bat Mitzvah day comes, the Torah scroll is symbolically passed from generation to generation—from grandparent to parent to child. The parent makes a brief statement before handing the Torah scroll to the child, who speaks briefly some words of personal acceptance. Subsequently, the child reads or chants the blessings over the Torah and reads part of the weekly portion, as well as a text from the Hebrew prophets. Customarily, the child leads the congregation in at least part of the worship service and expounds on the meaning of that week's Torah text for his or her life.

In my experience, the Bar/Bat Mitzvah ceremony is a powerful symbolic recognition that a child—no longer just a child—is entering a stage of greater religious responsibility as Bar Mitzvah, son of the Jewish deed, or Bat Mitzvah, daughter of the Jewish deed. The individual recognition to child and family in the presence of the congregation has an impact. Years later, when I teach the children in preparation for

Confirmation, many recall the Bar/Bat Mitzvah as a time when they felt closest to the God of the covenant.

There is a major problematic of Bar Mitzvah, especially for liberal Judaism. Ideally, this rite of passage signaled the age of responsibility for performing the *mitzvot* (commandments) of a covenant life. Henceforth it was incumbent upon the child to fast on Yom Kippur, to count for a quorum in a public worship service, no longer to expect parents to carry the full burden of *tzedekah* (charitable giving).

In reality, the Bar Mitzvah often consists of the ceremonial reading from the Torah scroll and leading the congregation in worship that day rather than constituting any palpable transition to a stage of greater Jewish responsibility. All too often, even among Orthodox and Conservative Jews, Bar Mitzvah does not significantly deepen the child's level of covenant witness. Frequently, it simply marks the end of formal religious training.

Among Reform congregations there is an additional theoretical obstacle. Reform Jews affirm a large measure of autonomy in determining which of the deeds address us as divine command. This freedom at times easily lapses into comfortable irresponsibility. The challenge is to retain the element of choice while encouraging a Bar Mitzvah and his family to mark this transition by tangibly choosing to deepen their pattern of Jewish ethical and ritual living.

Study of the Torah

We are told that "a little child shall lead them." That prophecy has been amply fulfilled. Many Jewish adults are drawn to synagogue affiliation by the awareness that their child is ready for religious instruction. Regrettably, Jewish education may become too child centered.

Parents are not always good models. They forget that they cannot easily transmit what they themselves do not possess. Nor can even the best religious school adequately compensate for a spiritually impoverished home. How demoralizing to teach religious-school children skills, such as reciting grace before meals, that are conspicuous by their absence at home! Even as a child learns most about love by observing the way his or her parents relate to each other, so the child learns most about Judaism by observing the Jewish living patterns within the family. Most synagogues have rather impressive opportunities for adult study, but most such programs reach a small proportion of the adult congregation.

Traditionally, Torah study used to be a lifelong pursuit. Classic is the image of a section of the synagogue, the *Beth Hamidrash*, the house of study, occupied by adults who, with or without a professional instructor, learned Torah together. It was deemed preferable to study that was under the leadership of a guide.

The highest form of study was *lishma*—study for its own sake. Such study was not intended to lead to ordination or even to a solution of a particular problem at hand, but to fulfill the mitzvah of learning "the laws of life," a way of drawing closer to the Giver of Torah.

Classic study for adults and children has been text oriented. The age of prophetic revelation has passed, but divine instruction and illumination are very real for the one who opens mind and heart to the meaning and nuances of sacred texts. To symbolize this ongoing teaching, the one who blesses the Torah recites the benediction "Praised be Thou, O Lord, who *gives* the Torah." In the daily liturgy, God is presented as "One who *teaches* Torah to His people Israel."

Classic study of the Torah involves a creative encounter between both student and teacher, and student and text. Rabbi Simeon ben Lakish notes that in Exodus 31 God gave Moses the tablets after "speaking *with* him." *With*, not *to*, stresses the rabbi. After the initial revelation, God, the primary Teacher, invited Moses to recite the teaching with God and thereby make the teaching his own.[13]

We need to own what we are taught. That sense derives

from an active, creative involvement in the learning process. In classic Jewish study the student is encouraged to become an active partner. There is no single, authoritative Jewish commentary to scripture. A classic text for study is surrounded by as many as a dozen marginal commentaries produced over a span of a thousand years or mo.e. The student notes that various rabbis thought differently about a text; so may he. As Martin Buber noted: "A generation can only receive the teachings in the sense that it renews them. We do not take unless we also give. In the living tradition it is not possible to draw a line between preserving and producing."[14]

One of the most exciting developments in contemporary adult Jewish education is a recovery of the study of texts. Since most American Jews are not able to handle texts in the original Hebrew or Aramaic, virtually all the major texts are available in English translation. Those who participate in regular group study of the texts, under the guidance of a rabbi or another teacher, have rediscovered the joy of learning how others have received the text and exploring how it may address them. In our congregation's weekly Sabbath Torah Study session there is often vigorous debate and, at times, poignant self-revelation as each searches for a truth in the text.

In recent years more adult Jews have sought an act of covenant renewal through an adult Bar Mitzvah. In preparation, they learn to read a portion of the Torah in the original Hebrew, study the Hebrew prayers as part of a curriculum in basic Jewish thought and practice, and, on the appointed weekend, jointly conduct the service, reaccept the Torah, and expound its meaning in the presence of the congregation. This may be the closest equivalent in contemporary Judaism to being "born again." Through programs of study culminating in a ceremony of recommitment, the congregants discover the special valence of religious education as they renew their bonds with the sacred.

The Rabbi as Teacher

To mediate this renewal is one of the primary functions of the rabbi (or cantor) as teacher. Milton Steinberg described the rabbi as a teacher of the tradition.

To say of rabbis that they are teachers is to deny that they are priests. Unlike some other religions, Judaism does not assert of its clergy that they possess spiritual powers . . . which are unavailable to the laity. . . . In the end the rabbi differs from his Jewish fellows only in being more learned than they, or more expert in the tradition they all share. He is a rabbi by virtue of education; his ordination is graduation, his title an academic degree.[15]

This definition hardly does justice to the rabbinic role. The rabbi is more than a teacher in the academic sense. His teaching has a priestly dimension. As rabbis, our blessing at a Bar Mitzvah or a wedding, or our affirmation of the significance of a human life at a funeral has special resonance because the rabbi is perceived as having dedicated his life to a covenant which proclaims the presence and power of God.

The priestly role imposes more burdens than privileges. We are not immune to doubt even as we are called to model faith. We are not immune to moral transgressions, yet our people need us more to model our virtues than our frailty. Again, Martin Buber's words are apt:

The teachings must not be treated as a collection of knowable materials. . . . Either the teachings live in the life of a responsible human being or they are not alive at all.[16]

Like parents to the young child, we rabbis are, by virtue of our rabbinic vocation, privileged to encounter persons at the most teachable moments of their lives. We teach not only in the classroom but in the counseling session, the hospital bedside, and at the grave. We are entrusted with precious echoes of the Torah's deepest truths as reflected in the stories of our people's lives. In our moments of grace as defenders of

the covenant, we feel moved to say, "Praised be Thou, O
Lord, ruling spirit of the universe, who has made us teachers
of Torah to the household of Israel."

Notes

1. *Midrash*, Deuteronomy Rabbah 2:35.
2. Martin Buber, *Israel and the World* (New York: Schocken
   Books, 1948), 137.
3. Israel Ibn Al Nakawa, "Concerning the Rearing of Children,"
   Menorat Ha-maor, ed. H. G. Enelow (New York: Bloch Publishing, 1932), 145.
4. Exodus Rabbah 28:2.
5. Buber, *Israel and the World*, 140.
6. Ibid., 144.
7. Allan Bloom, *The Closing of the American Mind* (New York:
   Simon and Schuster, 1987), 60–61.
8. *Palestinian Talmud*, Hagigah 1:7.
9. *Babylonian Talmud*, Sukkah 47a–b.
10. Ibid., Rosh Hashanah 33a.
11. Ibid., Yonea 82a.
12. See *A Passover Haggadah*, ed. Herbert Bronstein (New York:
    Central Conference of American Rabbis, 1982).
13. Exodus Rabbah 6:5.
14. Buber, *Israel and the World*, 139.
15. Milton Steinberg, *Basic Judaism* (New York: Harcourt, Brace &
    Co., 1947), 154–55.
16. Buber, *Israel and the World*, 140.

CHAPTER 4

The Teaching Function of Liturgy

Stanley Samuel Harakas

BEFORE DISCUSSING THE TEACHING FUNCTION OF LITURGY, I will try to place Eastern Orthodox Christianity in a historical frame of reference and picture its mind-set and style in broad brush strokes. I will indicate how the sources of its faith, that is, the scriptures and holy tradition, are embedded in its worship. I will then illustrate how moral and spiritual instruction takes place in Orthodox Christian worship life. A brief treatment of some Orthodox pastoral aspects of the teaching function of liturgy, both positive and negative, will follow. I will conclude with some suggestions of an ecumenical nature regarding the teaching function of the liturgy from the Eastern Orthodox perspective.

The Place and Ethos of Orthodoxy within Christianity

From personal experience, it seems to me that most Americans see Christianity as having two parts: Roman Catholic and Protestant. When I am introduced as a member of the clergy of the Eastern Orthodox Church, I often observe a valiant struggle to place me within that framework. Since I am not a Roman Catholic priest (I am married with five children), many seek to place me, by default, somewhere on that wide continuum of churchly realities known as Protestantism. But when others observe the sacerdotal and liturgical aspects of my priesthood—for example, the fact that people call me "Father," and that I use incense extensively in worship, or that I serve the Divine Liturgy in a full and complex set of vestments—they try to make an ersatz Roman Catholic out of me and say that the Orthodox are "just like the Catholics" except "you don't have the Pope, and you do have married priests."

This attempt at identification is doomed to failure, since Eastern Orthodox Christianity is neither Roman Catholic nor Protestant. We have an almost two-thousand-year tradition whose history, theology, liturgical life, spirituality, saintly figures, and vision are clearly distinguished from that of Roman Catholicism and Protestantism. From the perspective of Orthodox Christianity both Roman Catholicism and Protestantism are "Western," while Orthodox Christianity is "Eastern." The "West" is Latin, Frankish, and Germanic in its cultural matrix and roots; the "East" is Greek, Syrian, and Slavic in its cultural character.[1]

This was true long before the sharp break between the East and the West in A.D. 1054. Known as the "Great Schism," this division reflected the essential reality that tragically had come into being—that two major approaches to Christianity existed and for about a millennium have been traveling their separate ways.[2]

Orthodoxy emphasizes continuity with the past. It is not just historical traditionalism. Everything about the Orthodox Church seeks to keep in the forefront the eternal dimensions of the faith. The past is never conceived of as dead and gone. Rather, it is a living presence. For example, nearly all of the major feasts relating to the life of Christ include hymns that locate the event liturgically not in the past but in the present. Thus, at Christmas we sing, "Today, Christ is born"; on Great Friday we sing, "Today, Christ is hung upon the Cross";

during the Paschal season we sing, "Today, Death is overcome for Christ is risen."[3]

But the future is also made present in the liturgical life. The central act of worship for the Orthodox is the Divine Liturgy, the Sacrament of the Body and Blood of Jesus Christ. Orthodox theologians see it not primarily as a teaching occasion or the fulfillment of a spiritual obligation. Rather, they understand worship as a whole, and the Divine Liturgy in particular, as a "manifestation of the eternal Kingdom of God."[4] To participate properly in the Divine Liturgy means, in part, spiritually to leave Houston, or Boston, or New York for a while and to enter the eschatological reality of the kingdom of God.[5] This perspective is central. What is said below about the teaching function of liturgy is dependent upon it, and not the other way around.

The Eastern Church is called "Orthodox" by way of supporting its claim of holding and maintaining the original and authentic faith of the early undivided church, unchanged and undistorted. It is also called 'Orthodox because it senses that in its praise of God in time and space, in doctrine and hymn, in sacrament and service, in color and symbol, it is rooted in the mind-set and ethos of the ever-present living reality of the early Christian witness. For the Orthodox, persons such as Abraham, Moses, Peter, John, Paul, Athanasius of Alexandria, Basil of Cappadocia, John Chrysostom of Antioch and Constantinople, and above all, Christ the Savior, are not primarily historical figures. They are contemporaries. And it is in the worship experience of Orthodox Christianity that this is made most evident.

Much more could be said to place Orthodoxy vis-à-vis Western Christianity in terms of both history and ethos. Suffice it to say that in Orthodox Christianity the tonality is more corporate that individual, more internal than external, more spiritual than activist, more aesthetic than rational. It is governed more by relationships than by rules and procedures, captured more by the eschatological and eternal than by the concrete and ephemeral. These latter dimensions are not absent in Orthodox Christianity; they are simply not the controlling elements.

Gospel and Doctrine in Orthodox Worship

One of the interesting observations to be made about Orthodox worship is its dominantly corporate, objective, and theological character. To be sure, there are present in the huge corpus of Orthodox liturgical materials many expressions of personal faith and personal religious experience. The first person singular does make an occasional appearance in the hymnology of the church. However, the first person plural is much more frequently met. Even more striking, however, is the descriptive, matter-of-fact stating of Christian truth in Orthodox hymnology. For example, in the Divine Liturgy there is a hymn that can be described as a "little Christian creed." It reads as follows:

> Only begotten Son and Word of God, although immortal You humbled Yourself for our salvation, taking flesh from the holy Theotokos and ever-Virgin Mary and, without change, becoming man. Christ, our God, You were crucified but conquered Death by Your death. You are one of the Holy Trinity, glorified with the Father and the Holy Spirit—save us.[6]

Here the discerning observer will perceive the dependence of the hymn upon the narratives of the four Gospels, the "logos" theology of the Fourth Gospel, the Pauline focus upon the saving work of Jesus Christ, the trinitarian and incarnational theology of the early ecumenical councils, and the doxological character of Christian truth. The same observer will note that in the whole of this lengthy stanza there is only one petition. It expresses the only petition appropriate to this recounting of the core of the Christian faith: "Save us."[7] The didactic and instructive character of this representative hymn is clearly evident.

Another feature of Orthodox worship is the strong presence of the Bible. Scripture permeates its mindset, ethos, worship, and life style. Demetrios Constantelos has documented this reality. In "The Holy Scriptures in Greek Orthodox Worship, A Comparative and Statistical Study,"[8] he shows that in the fixed liturgical texts of the sacramental and nonsacramental services of the Orthodox Church, not only is the scripture read as text numerous times in most services, but it permeates the language of the prayers and the hymns themselves. Passages resonate with biblical phrases without formal quotation, and they re-present, interpret, and cultivate biblical images and symbols, as Jean Danielou has pointed out in his book *The Bible and Liturgy*.[9]

An example of the didactic and formative character of the lectionary readings is found in the Sundays that precede the beginning of the Paschal Lenten period. Beginning the period known as the *Triodion* (which is recorded in a service book of the same name, one of sixteen major service books for the church year),[10] there is a planned and defined course of spiritual and moral preparation presented for the edification of the faithful. The daily liturgical cycle, from the Vespers through Orthros (or Matins) and the occasional hymns in the Divine Liturgy for each of these four Sundays before Lent, is based on four selected biblical passages, supported by the hymns of the services and customarily by traditional preaching patterns.

The first Sunday of the *Triodion* is the Sunday of the Publican and the Pharisee, with its focus on the basic requirement of humility for spiritual growth. Contrasting this virtue is the need to put away pride and the aggrandizement of the ego.[11]

The following Sunday, the church presents the people with another parable, the story of the prodigal son, which is a dramatic call for repentence. Without constant repentance[12] there can be no spiritual growth.[13]

The sense of progression in teaching for preparation in the Lenten journey to the Paschal experience of the resurrection of Jesus Christ becomes clear when it is noted that the third Sunday of the *Triodion*, known as Meatfare Sunday (because it is the last day in which meat is to be eaten before the beginning of Great Lent), presents the congregation with the Matthean account of the last judgment. The dramatic separation of the sheep and the goats, not on the basis of faith, piety, prayer, or knowledge, but only on the basis of works of love for the suffering neighbor, clearly indicates that humility and repentance must bear fruit in loving Christian service to the Christ in every person who is in need.[14]

The final preparatory Sunday, known as both Cheesefare Sunday (because it is the last day in which dairy products are to be eaten) and Forgiveness Sunday, draws its scriptural reading from the Sermon on the Mount. The pedagogical intent associated with the beginning of the Lenten period is clearly evident when one notes that the segment selected from the Sermon on the Mount (Matt. 6:14–21) covers the Lord's teaching on forgiveness of others, the proper attitude when fasting, and the preference for spiritual rather than material treasures. The next day is Clean Monday, a strict fast day and the beginning of the Great Lent.

It is not hard to see how preaching, which is traditionally governed by the gospel lectionary, would serve to prepare the people for the proper approach to the Lenten experience. It promotes humility in the face of pride; it calls the believer to anticipate and expect change in his or her life through repentance; it challenges the believer to move out of restricted concern with the inner life to a life of loving service to those in need as an aspect of the Christian's relationship with the Lord; and, finally, it puts the Christian's values in order with ready forgiveness of others, giving a serious purpose to the fasting discipline as well as an emphasis on the importance of the spiritual side of Christian life and growth.

The rich hymnology for each of these Sundays reinforces

the message. One example is from the Vespers on the evening of Forgiveness Sunday, just before the Fast is to begin.

Let us set out with joy upon the season of the Fast, and prepare ourselves for spiritual combat. Let us purify our soul and cleanse our flesh; and as we fast from food, let us abstain from every sinful passion. Rejoicing in the virtues of the Spirit may we persevere with love, and so be counted worthy to see the solemn Passion of Christ our God, and with great spiritual gladness to behold His holy Passover.[15]

The liturgical sharing in the central meaning and events of the core of the gospel message thus becomes a profound and significant educational experience for the faithful parishioner who consciously and prayerfully participates in the worship of the church.

Moral and Spiritual Instruction in Orthodox Worship

In 1958, Evangelos Theodorou, professor of liturgical theology at the University of Athens, argued in *The Educational Value of the Triodion*[16] that the *Triodion* is structurally an educational book, that it is designed to create ways of life for the worshipers, and that it does this by drawing on Scripture and by being a "treasure house of Holy Tradition."[17] The first of his conclusions is this: "The Triodion—even though it does not have systematically formed and explicitly stated catechetical, educational and instructional purposes—possesses incomparable educational value, which flows from both its form and its content."[18]

I believe it would be possible to take any one of the major service books of the Orthodox liturgical cycle and study it carefully for its instructional value, as Professor Theodorou did with the *Triodion* in his book. I did the same thing a number of years ago in an article published in Greek with the title "The Ethical Teaching of the Pentekostarion,"[19] the liturgical book for the Easter period.

Further, the same exercise could take place in reference to

the sacraments in general, and in particular, baptism, the eucharist, marriage, and confession. A similar treatment showing the educational and instructional dimensions of each of the Lenten Sundays, every day in Holy Week, Easter, Pentecost, Christmas, the feasts of nearly all of the saints, and occasional services such as the bread-blessing service, the water-blessing service, and the funeral service, among others, could also be done rather readily.[20] For example, premarital counseling in the Orthodox Church nearly always includes extensive reference to the text and liturgical practices of the Sacrament of Holy Matrimony.

To illustrate more specifically the educative character of Orthodox worship and liturgical practice, we can first examine the hymnology of one minor feast, "The Presentation of Jesus at the Temple," and then seek to understand the instructional dimension of icons as used in the Orthodox Church.

The Feast of the Presentation of Jesus at the Temple

The Gospel of Luke is the only Gospel to describe the presentation of Jesus at the temple. Fulfilling the requirements of the Jewish ritual law regarding the firstborn son of every Jewish family meant that on the fortieth day following the baby's birth, the parents were to bring the child to the temple in Jerusalem, where a modest sacrifice of "a pair of turtledoves or two young pigeons" was to be offered. Joseph and Mary fulfill the "custom of the law" and bring the infant Jesus to the temple. The event takes on soteriological and messianic dimensions when the righteous and holy Symeon, guided by the Holy Spirit, recognizes the Christchild as the Messiah, lifts him up in his hands, and says, "Mine eyes have seen thy salvation, which thou hast prepared in the presence of all peoples, a light for revelation to the Gentiles, and for glory to thy people Israel" (Luke 2:30–32).

Symeon follows this doxology with a dramatic prediction regarding the impact of the child on the future of Israel. The aged prophetess Anna is presented as speaking about Jesus "to all who were looking for the redemption of Jerusalem." The passage is found in Luke 2:22–38. Counting forty days from Christmas, the feast is celebrated on February 2. It is a source of both rich, beautiful, and instructive hymnology, and a powerfully instructive popular liturgical practice.

Samples of the hymnology can only be illustrative of the whole instructive tone of the feast. I present the following texts with a minimum of commentary, for I think they speak eloquently enough for themselves.

In the Vespers, on the eve of the Feast of the Presentation, the sacred poet enters into dialogue with Symeon and uses the dialogue to lift up the saving implications of the event and to personalize them.[21]

> Say, O Symeon, whom carriest thou in the Temple in thine arms with rejoicing? Towards whom dost thou cry, shouting, Now I have been let to depart; for I have beheld my Saviour. This is he born of the Virgin. This is the Word, God of God, who was incarnate for our sakes and saved humanity. Him let us worship.

There is not just a rehearsing of the biblical narrative here; it is made alive and given theological content, and from it one imperative is drawn: "Him let us worship." From the Orthros, or Matins service, further instruction is conveyed and cast in quite personal terms. Hearing it, the worshiper cannot help but be drawn into the saving work of Christ. Its instructive character becomes formative. The focus is Christ as the source of true life.

> Verily, the Ancient of Days becometh a babe for my sake; and the all-pure God shareth in the impure to save me in the flesh which he took from the Virgin. And Symeon, having been made confidant to these mysteries, knew him as God appearing in the flesh. Wherefore he kissed him; for he is the Life; and the old man cried with joy saying, Lettest thou me depart; for I have beheld thee, O Life of all.

At the end of the Orthros service is a set of hymns known as the "Praises," or *Ainoi*. In these there is more material that can be considered to have instructional character. In the doxological mode of Orthodox worship, themes of Christ as the sun of justice and the light of revelation are presented. The sacred poet gives a spiritual nuance to Symeon's declaration that he was free to depart from this world now that he had seen the Savior.

> O Lord, Sun of righteousness, thou hast appeared as a light for the revelation of the Gentiles, sitting on a bright cloud, fulfilling the shadowy law and revealing the beginning of the new grace. Wherefore, when Symeon beheld thee he lifted his voice, crying, Lettest thou me depart from corruption; for I have today beheld thee.

This same didactic, declarative tone is present in other hymns of the Feast of the Presentation which, in a favorite manner, find parallels between the events of the feast and teachings to be seen in them. Thus, the simple holding of the child by the aged man becomes an occasion to affirm a truth about God. In one of the hymns we read, "Lord, thou wast delivered into the hands of Symeon, the God-receiver, O thou who holdest all creation in thy hand."

Hymns, of course, are not just words. They are music as well. Orthodox ecclesiastical music is based on ancient Christian musical systems with eight distinct musical tones, each of which can be sharped and flatted. Each tone has its distinctive emotional character, and each, with its melodies, is capable of conveying the spirit of the hymn texts. Constantine Cavarnos writes:

> The aim of Byzantine sacred music is spiritual. This music is, in the first place, a means of worship and veneration; and in the second place, a means of self-perfection, of eliciting and cultivating man's higher thoughts and feelings and of opposing and eliminating his lower, undesirable ones.

He continues:

There is not one kind of music employed as a means of worshipping God and honoring the saints, and another kind employed for transforming our inner life, but the same music, which having as its direct aim the former, incidentally leads also the fulfillment of the latter. For while glorifying God and honoring the saints by means of psalms and hymns, or while listening to others chant while we do so in our hearts, feelings such as sadness, hatred, anger, and torpor subside, and feelings such as contrition, love, peace and spiritual joy and aspiration are aroused.[22]

Cavarnos quotes Niketas Stethatos, the eleventh-century hegoumen (abbot) of the Studite Monastery of Constantinople, as saying:

Now the quality of psalmody and prayer depends on praying with the spirit and the mind; and one prays with the mind, when, in praying and psalmodizing, one observes carefully the mind that is contained in the Divine Scripture and thence receives uplifting ideas into his heart from divine meanings.[23]

A touching and almost naive use of music and words is to be found in the set of hymns known as the "Megalynaria" from the Orthros service of the Feast of the Presentation. The image of the Christchild being held in the arms of the Virgin Mother and in the arms of the righteous Symeon provoked the creator of this set of hymns to form it into a gentle lullaby. Not only is the story of the event told but the "divine meanings," to use Niketas Stethatos's words, are articulated in a simple and guileless musical setting that disarms sophisticated pretensions and opens the door for the kind of gentle influence mentioned above. One not only visualizes but feels Mary's motherly tenderness and Symeon's gentleness as they rock the child gently in their arms. The words of the text slip almost unnoticed into our minds and our hearts. Here is a small segment of the text of the "Megalynaria" for the Feast of the Presentation of the Christchild at the temple.

That which is fulfilled in you
Is beyond understanding
Of angels and mortal man
O pure Virgin Mother.

Symeon the Elder
Takes in his arms today
The Maker of the law
And master of all.

The Creator wishing
To save Adam
Took up his dwelling in
Your pure and virgin womb.

All mankind blesses you
O pure virgin
And in faith glorifies
You as Mother of God.

Come, you and behold
Christ the Master of all,
Whom Symeon holds
In the Temple today.[24]

Icons as Instructive

In Orthodox Christianity, painted or mosaic representations of holy persons and events are widely used in the church. Known as icons, they are not thought of as simple pictures. The teaching regarding icons was formalized, after centuries of debate, in the seventh ecumenical council, held in A.D. 787 in Nicaea. The icon, through its unique style, color, shape, and placement, is understood not as being representative of the external features of the person or event depicted but as revealing the inner, spiritual, heavenly, and sanctified aspects of that person or event.

The icon is presented as having, in addition, a kind of

impress and influence upon the believer. In fact, precisely as icon and not as mere picture, the icon is seen as serving a purpose of formation of the viewer, not based on subjective emotions or imaginations but upon the objective divine-human reality which the Christian is called to realize in life. Its purpose is not only to inform but to form the heart, mind, will, and life of the believer.

The function of the icon to provoke imitation toward virtue is most clearly seen in St. John of Damascus's three homilies on the divine images, which were written in the eighth century. Two of the many passages follow:

> Things which have already taken place are remembered by means of icons, whether for the purpose of inspiring wonder, or honor, or shame, or to encourage those who look upon them to practice good and avoid evil.[25]

> I bow down before the icons of Christ, the incarnate God; of our Lady, the Theotokos and Mother of the Son of God; and of the saints, who are God's friends. In struggling against evil they have shed their blood; they have imitated Christ who shed His Blood for them by shedding their blood for Him. I make a record of the prowess and sufferings of those who have walked in His footsteps, that I may be sanctified, and be set on fire to imitate them zealously.[26]

Modern Orthodox writers thus have affirmed the didactic character of the icon, an emphasis that points toward the worshiping viewer and to the divine. Even abbreviated accounts of the icon, such as that of Bishop Timothy Ware, in his very popular introduction, *The Orthodox Church,* make mention of the didactic character of the icons for the people of God.[27]

But even more detailed studies of iconography do the same. Daniel J. Sahas, in *Icon and Logos: Sources in Eighth Century Iconoclasm*[28] eloquently points to the didactic nature of the icon. Thus, he says that icons

serve to "articulate"; and accentuate the word of the Scriptures
and the theology of the Church. They serve as a means of
spiritual elevation and an instrument of instruction, not only
for the illiterate, but even for the literate ones who want,
however, to penetrate beyond the realm of the word and reason. . . . As the word became a means of instruction through
hearing, so did the icon through vision.[29]

He quotes the famous Greek iconographer Fotis Kontoglou,
who says that the icons "do not aim only at decorating a
church with paintings in order for it to be aesthetically attractive and pleasant to the worshippers, . . . but rather in order
to elevate them to the mystical world of faith."[30]

As an example, one could point to the traditional Byzantine
icon of the resurrection of Christ, in which Christ is presented
as breaking the bounds of hell. He stands victoriously upon
the gates of hell. Broken and fragmented locks and keys are
scattered at his feet. Concurrently, he stretches out his hands
to the left and to the right, grasping the outstretched hands of
two figures, Adam and Eve, whom he draws out of the tombs
in which they have been lying. It should not surprise anyone
that this icon is frequently used by Orthodox priests to interpret the meaning of the Paschal feast to their congregations, in
particular, to the children.

The Effectiveness of Liturgical Education

I cannot say that the vast liturgical resources of Orthodoxy,
including all that I have described here, are fully and adequately used for the education and enrichment of the faithful.
Liturgical education does take place, without question. In
addition to what has been mentioned above, it is true that the
power of the liturgical and cultic life to educate and form
people for Christian thinking, Christian living, and in Christian attitudes continues. I think of the impact of the rites of
Holy Week in the Orthodox Church, for example. This whole

essay could have been built on the formative influence of the week-long series of services for Holy Week, which allow the Christian to relive the last days of the earthly life of Christ. In the Orthodox Church, Holy Week is a liturgical passion play.

As indicated above, each of these days is made, liturgically, into a present reality. The believer is present at the Last Supper on Holy Thursday. The unjust condemnation and crucifixion of Jesus is experienced, one might say, firsthand in the "Service of the Twelve Gospels," the Matins (Orthros) service of Great Friday. The believers observe the agony of the cross and the descent of the holy body of Christ from the cross at the Good Friday vespers. The faithful literally attend the "wake," or "viewing," of Jesus and sing songs of lamentation and mourning at the side of his coffin. They accompany him in solemn procession to the place of burial at the Orthros of Holy Saturday. They remember prophetic words of victory over death, sin, and evil at the vesperal liturgy that follows. In the hour before midnight, toward the dawn of Easter, they gather in hushed and solemn anticipation in a darkened church for the first word which proclaims the ever old yet forever new and exciting announcement "Christ is risen!" And as if with one voice, all respond in joyous acclamation, "Truly, he is risen!"

How can one not be formed by such experiences! Yet, sadly, over the centuries many forces have been at work that have blunted the power of the liturgy to educate. Several decades ago the late Father Alexander Schmemann addressed the contemporary problems of Orthodoxy. In an insightful article titled "The Liturgical Problem," he spoke of the purpose of worship, and he assessed the present state of affairs. His central concern was

> the *power* of the liturgy, first, to impress on the soul of man the Orthodox vision of life, and second, to help him live in accordance with that vision. Or, to put it in simple terms, the influence of the liturgy on our ideas, decisions, behavior, evaluations—on the totality of our life.

He continued, so pertinently for this inquiry on the educative function of liturgy, affirming that

> this was for centuries and centuries the real function of the liturgy in the Orthodox Church: to immerse man in the spiritual reality, beauty and depth of the Kingdom of God, and to *change* his mind and his heart.[31]

His assessment about the status of the educative and formative function of worship was, however, very pessimistic. He said in 1963: "Today, however, this power of worship has all but vanished. Worship is something one must attend and even enjoy, it is a self-evident 'obligation' for the religious man, but it has lost all relevance for the real life."[32] In his treatment of the problem, Father Alexander addressed issues such as language, translation, parish structure and purpose, concern with rubrics, and problems related to the various families of liturgical rites. And it is true that, for the Orthodox who have come to the United States from many different lands with strong ethnic and linguistic traditions, the issue of language is important. Younger people are often impatient with conservative attitudes that struggle to maintain the mother tongue in worship. In some places, and in some of the Orthodox ethnic jurisdictions, English now predominates in worship. In others, a policy of "flexible bilingualism" is dominant. Yet such issues, in Schmemann's view, are not central. At the heart of the problem he finds the secularistic attitude that had been absorbed by many in the Church. In other words, he found an issue of faith. Genuine worship cannot take place without well-placed faith.

Perhaps Schmemann overdramatized the issue. Nevertheless, there was truth in what he said. Others also sensed the need for a reawakening of liturgical understanding. In the past twenty-five years, vigorous efforts have been made in Orthodox Christianity to increase overall sensitivity in the church to its liturgical resources. The seriousness of the concern has been emphasized repeatedly by the Orthodox since the sixties.

Theological statements regarding the need to cultivate the liturgical life have been repeatedly made in pan-Orthodox ecumenical meetings. One example is from the Orthodox Consultation on Education in the Orthodox Church, held in Utrecht, Holland, in 1972. In part, the Orthodox representatives there said: "Many Orthodox leaders, theologians and educators are struggling for renewal in their churches. The increasing emphasis on the liturgical sermon and on full participation in liturgical life is contributing to renewal in Orthodox Churches today."[33]

Another example is from the Orthodox Consultation on "Confessing Christ Today" in Bucharest, Romania, in 1974. In the third report, the seriousness of the need for increased sensitivity to the message of liturgy was underlined.

> The Beauty of the Liturgy educates our hearts and our eyes to the contemplation of the uncreated light of the Holy Trinity in its heavenly glory. But if the Glory of the Cross and the Divine Beauty of the Liturgy do not transfigure our own sinful ugliness into real internal Beauty our participation in the Liturgy leads to our judgment and condemnation.

To this was added a further affirmation of the formative and even evangelistic power of the Divine Liturgy.

> Though the Divine Liturgy is essentially and primarily the realization of the unity of the Church with Christ, and as such is in and of itself a manifestation of the reality of the Church, it may have consequences for the Evangelistic Witness of the Church. From all parts of the world we bring witness to the transforming and evangelizing power of the Divine Liturgy.[34]

In 1974 I published a book titled *Living the Liturgy,* whose purpose it is to encourage lay participation in the Divine Liturgy.[35] After fourteen years it is still in print and still widely distributed. Father Schmemann's writings on the eucharist, baptism, and other services continue to provoke changes of understanding and liturgical apprehension among the Orthodox.[36]

A veritable river of publications has served to move the Church to a deeper appreciation and understanding of its liturgical heritage. An example is a series of volumes issued by Arkritas publishers in Greece, each on a single feast of the church. For example, part of the ongoing series includes volumes on Christmas[37] and on the Feast of the Transfiguration.[38] There is a volume titled *Cross and Resurrection*[39] and one titled *Pentecost: From the Resurrection to the Church*.[40] Each volume affirms the educative function of liturgy. For example, in the last of the above-mentioned books, we read:

> When reference is made in the liturgical life of the Church regarding publicans and pharisees, prodigal sons, prostitutes, and the palsied, about lawyers and blind-men, we customarily feel that all these things refer to other people and that fortunately we are not included in these categories. But the liturgical climate of the Church strongly emphasizes the opposite, that all of them are all of us.[41]

All these statements are indicative of the felt need of the Orthodox to improve the liturgical comprehension of the faithful and to draw on their liturgical resources for the education and formation of their own people.

An Ecumenical Suggestion

Of course, the issues of liturgical renewal also have been strongly emphasized recently in Western Christianity. The post-Vatican II revolution in liturgical practice in the Roman Catholic Church is well known. The involvement of the World Council of Churches in the "Baptism-Eucharist-Ministry" studies has its liturgical side as well. The question is whether the strong liturgical tradition of Orthodox Christianity, especially in its educative and formative impact, has anything to say to Western Christians. I believe that the issue is a bit complex.

I have seen worship distorted into a propaganda device, into a totally this-worldly effort at influencing public opinion, especially in some Protestant academic settings. I must say, as an Orthodox, that something inside me rebels against such distortions of liturgy. This instrumentalist approach seems to say that the primary focus of worship is the influencing of the captive congregation, the "education" of them in the passing and ephemeral agenda of the person or group planning the service. Something about this manipulative approach to worship strips it of its very heart.

I can illustrate this from some comments made by a Baptist minister in Massachusetts who, writing recently in an article on "The Free Church and Art," complained that the "horizontally structured free churches" may in fact be subject to a "tyranny of the common," whose worship is "designed primarily to suit the mood of the congregation."[42] He wrote:

> The horizontally oriented free church differs from the more vertically organized churches in that in the latter there is a dependence on a liturgy which if not traced directly to God, is at least related to the ages, and to a "given" revelation. Obviously, liturgical churches have their serious problems, too, but it is fair to say that at least the intention of the liturgy is not designed to suit the mood of the congregation.[43]

Nor, I would add, is the intention of the liturgy primarily for propaganda purposes, whether it be religious, social, ethical, or political. While Orthodox Christians may have been learning ecumenically to rediscover in their own tradition the genuine didactic and instructive elements of worship, they are far from abandoning the essential "vertical" perspective of worship. For example, though the icon does have an instructive aspect to it, as we have seen, the icon is *primarily* a "window on heaven," a pointer to the heavenly, the divine, the transcendent, the spiritual. It does not exist *primarily* as propaganda or even as an educative device. It exists to bring us into communion with that reality which transcends us, yet which, paradoxically, is the source of the fullness of our humanity, and which, in the last analysis, makes human living possible.

Worship must in the first instance be anagogic; that is, it must be leading up-ward and God-ward, and down-ward and earth-ward. For worship to be worship, it does not suffice for it simply to draw on religious themes or provide religious sanction or color to secular ideas and interests. Constantine Cavarnos, in speaking of icons, is also speaking of worship when he says, "Its mode of expression must be spiritual, that is, such as to make it *anagogic*, pointing to a reality beyond the physical, lifting those who see it to a higher level of thought, feeling and consciousness, denoted by the term spiritual."[44]

What does this mean for some post-Vatican Roman Catholics and many free-church Protestants? It means that if the educative function of liturgy is, in fact, to accomplish its task properly, the order of priorities has to be reversed. Worship must point first heavenward. It must lead believers first and foremost into postures and attitudes of adoration before God. It must genuinely seek to convey the sense of the *Sanctus* before it undertakes the task of formation and education. In the Orthodox Divine Liturgy, the *Sanctus* hymn takes the tonality of awe and repentance: "Holy God, Holy Mighty One, Holy Immortal One, have mercy on us." It is instructive that in the structure of the Orthodox Divine Liturgy, this hymn is repeated again and again, just prior to the reading of the Epistle and the Gospel and the traditional place for the preaching of the sermon.[45]

So, while here I have largely sought to uncover the genuine tradition of liturgical instruction and teaching in the Orthodox Church, it must always be seen as a secondary function of liturgy. It is clear that in an ecumenical context the traditional heavy emphasis on the mystical and transcendent among the Orthodox has demanded a rediscovery of and even a reemphasis on the teaching function of the liturgy. However, for Western Christians, this moment in history may be requiring just the opposite.

What may be needed among Western Christians is a return to the objective, transcendent faith affirmations in revealed truth and to a worship style that is characterized by adoration and repentance before the living God. If this occurs, the teaching function of worship may once again be effective. It may be that as both East and West provide correctives to each other in their emphases in worship, they may meet and discover that their differences are fewer as a result of their separate journeys.

Conclusion

My first parish assignment was in Lancaster, Pennsylvania, in the mid-1950s. Several years after I undertook my duties in Lancaster, Dr. James E. Wagner, formerly the president of the Evangelical and Reformed Church and then the president of the newly formed United Church of Christ, visited the island of Rhodes in Greece. On Friday, September 4, 1959, the Lancaster *Daily Intelligencer Journal* carried an article describing his visit, including attendance at the Divine Liturgy of the Cathedral Church of the Annunciation. Dr. Wagner's personal involvement in Orthodox worship was a witness to the importance of liturgical understanding and the effect of liturgical learning; but most of all, it was an illustration of the way worship conveys its message.

I conclude with his description of that experience, written almost thirty years ago but an accurate summary nonetheless of what I have written here.

Two things made our participation in this service somewhat more intelligent than it might otherwise have been. Archbishop James (Iakovos), recently appointed head of the Greek Archdiocese of North and South America, provided each person with a small handbook, Greek and English on opposite pages, containing the text of the Liturgy of St. John Chrysostom which was used in the service. . . . I felt somewhat pleased that I could follow the service pretty well in Greek.

It was truly a "liturgy," which means literally a "service of the people." They participate many times and in many ways observably, the devout no doubt participating even more fully in ways unseen.

The choir really "assisted" the priest, and its "special music" was integral to the service itself, not, as is often true in Protestant churches, an artistic (if not artificial or even "arty") interlude.

There was an impact of awe and wonder, begetting a childlike trust which this service invokes in the minds and hearts of the devout. There is a crescendo character to the movement of this service which must, for the believer who is at home in it, carry him to devotional heights by the time the Communion is reached, and the Benediction pronounced.

Notes

1. For a full discussion of the cultural dimensions of Christianity in the East and the West, see Deno John Geanakopoulos, *Byzantine East and Latin West: Two Worlds of Christendom in the Middle Ages and Renaissance. Studies in Ecclesiastical and Cultural History* (New York: Barnes & Noble, 1966); idem, *Interaction of the "Sibling" Byzantine and Western Cultures in the Middle Ages and Italian Renaissance (330–1600)* (New Haven: Yale Univ. Press, 1976). For scholarly treatments of the Orthodox doctrine and ethos by Western scholars, see Jaroslav Pelikan, *The Spirit of Eastern Christendom (600–1700)* (Chicago: University of Chicago Press, 1977); J. M. Hussey, *The Orthodox Church in the Byzantine Empire* (Oxford: Clarendon Press, 1986). For briefer, more popular treatments, see Aristeides Papadakis, "History of the Orthodox Church," and Robert G. Stephanopoulos, "The Inter-Church Relations of the Orthodox Church," in *A Companion to the Greek Orthodox Church*, ed. Fotios K. Litsas (Dept. of Communications, Greek

Orthodox Archdiocese of North and South America, 1984), chaps. 2 and 9.

2. Important studies on the Great Schism between Eastern and Western Christendom include Francis Dvornik, *The Photian Schism: History and Legend* (Cambridge: Cambridge University Press, 1948); Philip Sherrard, *The Greek East and the Latin West* (London: Oxford University Press, 1959). For a brief account from the Eastern perspective, see Timothy Ware, *The Orthodox Church* (Baltimore: Penguin Books, 1972), chap. 3.

3. For the text of the Christmas hymns in English, see *Festal Menaion*, trans. Mother Mary and Archimandrite Kallistos Ware (Winchester, Mass.: Faber & Faber, 1977), sect. 4. For Great Friday hymns in English, see *The Lenten Triodion*, trans. Mother Mary and Archimandrite Kallistos Ware (Winchester, Mass.: Faber & Faber, 1978), 565–621. For the text of the Paschal services, see *Divine Prayers and Services of the Catholic Orthodox Church of Christ*, comp. Seraphim Nassar (Englewood, N.J.: Antiochian Orthodox Christian Archdiocese, 1979), 920–38. For a detailed presentation of the concept of "today" in Orthodox worship, see George Nicozisin, *The Road to Orthodox Phronema* (Brookline, Mass.: Dept. of Religious Education, Greek Orthodox Archdiocese, 1977), 86–89.

4. This perspective on Orthodox worship was extensively developed by the late Alexander Schmemann in *For the Life of the World*, 2d rev. ed. (Tuckahoe, N.Y.: St. Vladimir's Seminary Press, 1973); *Of Water and the Spirit: A Study on Baptism* (Tuckahoe, N.Y.: St. Vladimir's Seminary Press, 1974); *Introduction to Liturgical Theology*, 2d ed., trans. Asheleigh E. Moorehouse (Tuckahoe, N.Y.: St. Vladimir's Seminary Press, 1975); and *The Eucharist: Sacrament of the Kingdom* (Tuckahoe, N.Y.: St. Vladimir's Seminary Press, 1988).

5. See Alexander Schmemann, *Liturgy and Life: Lectures and Essays on Christian Development Through Liturgical Experience* (New York: Dept. of Religious Education, Orthodox Church in America, 1974); idem, *Great Lent*, rev. ed. (Tuckahoe, N.Y.: St. Vladimir's Seminary Press, 1974); and Stanley S. Harakas, *Living the Liturgy* (Minneapolis: Light and Life Pub. Co., 1974).

6. *The Divine Liturgy of Saint John Chrysostom: A New Transla-*

tion by Members of the Faculty of Hellenic College/Holy Cross Greek Orthodox School of Theology (Brookline, Mass.: Holy Cross Orthodox Press, 1985), 6, slightly revised.

7. Thus, "only begotten Son of God" (John 3:18); "Word of God" (John 1:1); "immortal" (1 Tim. 1:17, 6:16); "humbled Yourself" (Phil. 2:8); "for our salvation" (1 Thess. 5:9); "taking flesh" (John 1:14); "the holy Theotokos and ever-Virgin Mary" (Luke 1, 2; Gal. 4:4); "without change, becoming man" (2 Corinthians 4:4); "you were crucified" (1 Cor. 1:23, 2:2); "but conquered" (John 16:33); "Death by your death" (Rom. 6:9; 1 Cor. 15:26); "one of the Holy Trinity" (Phil. 2:6); "glorified with the Father" (John 14:13; 1 John 5:7). It is interesting to compare the hymn with early credal statements such as the Tome of Leo, accepted as Orthodox in the Fourth Ecumenical Council, as well as the decision (dogmatic "oros") of the council. See Documents of the Christian Church, ed. Henry Bettenson (New York: Oxford University Press, 1961), 68–73.

8. Demetrios Constantelos, "The Holy Scriptures in Greek Orthodox Worship, A Comparative and Statistical Study," Greek Orthodox Theological Review 12, no. 1 (1966): 80.

9. Jean Danielou, The Bible and Liturgy (Ann Arbor, Mich.: Servant Books, 1979).

10. This small liturgical library consists of the Horologion (daily services), the Parakletike (eight different resurrectional weekly rubrics, based on the eight tones of church music), the twelve Menaia (one for each month), the Triodion (Lent), and the Pentekostarion (the Paschal period).

11. Sixteenth Sunday of Luke, Luke 18:10–14.

12. Christoforos Stavropoulos, Partakers of Divine Nature, trans. Stanley S. Harakas (Minneapolis: Light and Life Publishing Co., 1979), 49–56.

13. Seventeenth Sunday of Luke, Luke 15:11–32.

14. Matt. 25:31–46.

15. The Lenten Triodion, trans. Mother Mary and Archimandrite Kallistos Ware (Winchester, Mass.: Faber & Faber, 1978), 181, slightly revised.

16. In Greek, "He Morphotike Axia tou Ischyontos Triodiou: Symboule eis ten Praktiken Theologian" (Athens: n.p. 1958).

17. Ibid., Book One, b, 1 and 2, pp. 44–68.

18. Ibid., 163.
19. "He Ethike Didaskalia tou Pentekostariou," *Theologia* 39 (July-September 1968): 368–85; and (October-December 1968): 586–612.
20. *An Orthodox Prayer Book*, ed. N. M. Vaporis; trans. John von Holzhausen and Michael Gelsinger (Brookline, Mass.: Holy Cross Orthodox Press, 1977).
21. All passages quoted below are from the translation of the Presentation services in *Divine Prayers and Services of the Catholic Orthodox Church of Christ*, comp. Seraphim Nassar (Englewood, N.J.: Antiochian Orthodox Christian Archdiocese, 1979), 494–510, slightly revised.
22. Constantine Cavarnos, *Byzantine Sacred Music* (Belmont, Mass.: Institute for Byzantine and Modern Greek Studies, 1956), 10.
23. Ibid., 25. Cavarnos indicates that he drew this reference from the collection of monastic spiritual writings known as the *Philokalia*.
24. Mother Mary and Archimandrite Kallistos Ware, *Festal Menaion*, 425–28.
25. Saint John of Damascus, *On Divine Images: Three Apologies Against Those Who Attack the Divine Images*, trans. David Anderson (Tuckahoe, N.Y.: St. Vladimir's Seminary Press, 1980), "First Apology," 13, 21.
26. Ibid., 21:29. Translations slightly modified.
27. Timothy Ware, *The Orthodox Church* (Baltimore: Penguin Books, 1963), 40–41.
28. Daniel J. Sahas, *Icon and Logos: Sources in Eighth Century Iconoclasm* (Toronto: University of Toronto Press, 1986).
29. Ibid., 12, 13.
30. Ibid.
31. Alexander Schmemann, "Problems of Orthodoxy in America: The Liturgical Problem," *St. Vladimir's Seminary Quarterly* 8, no. 3 (1964): 165.
32. Ibid.
33. Constantin G. Patelos, ed., *The Orthodox Church in the Ecumenical Movement: Documents and Statements 1902–1975* (Geneva: World Council of Churches, 1978), 102.
34. Ibid., 108, 112.

35. Stanley S. Harakas, *Living the Liturgy* (Minneapolis: Light and Life Publishing Co., 1974).
36. Schmemann, *For the Life of the World* and *Of Water and the Spirit.*
37. *Christougenna*, ed. Kostis Kyriakides (Athens: Akritas Publishing House, 1985).
38. *Metamorphose*, ed. Kostis Kyriakides (Athens: Akritas Publishing House, 1984).
39. *Stauros kai Anastase*, ed. Kostis Kyriakides (Athens: Akritas Publishing House, 1984).
40. *Pentekoste: Apo ten Anastase sten Ekklesia*, ed. Dina Hatze et al. (Athens: Akritas Publishing House, 1983).
41. Ibid., 55.
42. Norman de Puy, "The Free Church and Art," *Cabbages and Kings: A Commonplace Book* (January 1988).
43. Ibid., 2.
44. Constantine Cavarnos, "Byzantine Iconography," *Theologia* (1972), 9.
45. For the classic statement of this perspective, see Evelyn Underhill, *Worship* (New York: Harper & Brothers, 1937).

CHAPTER 5

A Moral Magisterium in Ecumenical Perspective

Richard A. McCormick, S.J.

I HAVE BEEN TEACHING MORAL THEOLOGY FOR THIRTY years. During that time I think it is fair to say that on no single issue have I heard more misstatements and more misunderstanding than on the teaching office in the Catholic church— the magisterium. Such misstatements are especially frequent in the area of morals, and often enough they center around the notion of infallibility. Thus it is distressingly common to hear, even from Catholics, expressions of surprise when a theologian, bishop, or priest qualifies a recent statement of the pope or of the Congregation for the Doctrine of the Faith. Somehow or other, Catholics are not supposed to do that. "After all, Father, is not the pope infallible when he addresses questions of faith and morals?" "How can you, as a Catholic, disagree with the official teachers?" "What good is the magisterium if Catholics are free to disagree with it?" The stereotypes are endless.

108   RICHARD A. McCORMICK, S.J.

Two Approaches to the Magisterium

This questioning is ecumenically important because the Petrine office is itself something of a stumbling block to many non-Catholics. This office—in its teaching function—may be approached in two ways. When it is conceived and presented in a narrow, rigid way, the stumbling block looms even larger. This narrow way is not entirely the product of popular misconceptions. There can be powerful reinforcements for it at very high levels. When Joseph Cardinal Ratzinger disallows in principle any dissent from noninfallible but authoritative church teaching, he is clearly choosing this way. This has been done in the now notorious case of Charles E. Curran of Catholic University. Curran has repeatedly argued that his dissent centers around noninfallible teachings. As he notes:

> The central issue involved in the controversy between the CDF and myself is the possibility of public theological dissent from some noninfallible teaching which is quite remote from the core of the faith, heavily dependent on support from human reason, and involved in such complexity and specificity that logically one cannot claim absolute certitude.[1]

Ratzinger denies this argument by deflating the distinction between infallible and noninfallible teaching. "The Church," he says, "does not build its life upon its infallible magisterium alone but on the teaching of its authentic, ordinary magisterium as well."[2] The implication of this statement is that whatever the church builds its life upon is not a proper matter for public dissent. That contention is, I believe, theologically and historically unsupportable. Ratzinger's sweeping negation led ecclesiologist Francis Sullivan, S.J., to remark, "The idea that Catholic theologians, at any level of education, can only teach the official church position and present only those positions in their writings, is new and disturbing."[3]

I agree that it is disturbing. But how new it is is a matter that can be discussed. Yves Congar, O.P., the great ecclesiologist and historian of dogma, wrote in 1976:

In point of fact, as the "ordinary magisterium" of popes has been exercized by excellent pontiffs in an incredible flow of encyclicals, speeches, and various interjections, this magisterium has assumed preponderant importance and, in the light of an intense "devotion to the pope," has been almost assimilated, in current opinion, to the prerogatives of the extraordinary magisterium. Besides, Pius XII, who carried it to its furthest point, expressed in the encyclical *Humani generis* (Aug. 12, 1950) his position on two points of great importance: (1) The ordinary magisterium of the pope requires total obedience. "He who listens to you listens to me." When the pope has expressed his *sententia* on a point previously controversial, there can no longer be any question of free discussion between theologians.[4] (2) The (or a) role of theologians is to justify the declarations of the magisterium.[5]

Thus rather clearly Pius XII would not justify public dissent against noninfallible teaching.

This view is still propounded by some Catholics of a quite conservative stripe. For instance, Joseph Farraher, S.J., argues that "professors at Catholic universities and seminaries . . . are considered and are representatives of the Church and as such should not promote opinions contrary to the teaching of the magisterium."[6] If dissenters feel that they must propose contradictory opinions, they should resign. If they persist, all efforts should be made to remove them. Kenneth Baker, S.J., goes even further. Theologians who "refuse to submit to the magisterium of the Church" should, after adequate dialogue, be excommunicated.[7]

Such views are frontal assaults on the viability of the notion of the magisterium in the contemporary world. They kill the patient while attempting to bandage a perceived wound. They are, however, minority, even if persistent, views.

Much more characteristic of mainstream Catholicism is the second approach characterized by the perspectives of Bishop Juan Arzube. He notes that, in contrast to infallible teaching, ordinary teaching has sometimes to "undergo correction and change." As an example, Arzube offers *Dignitatis humanae* and the teaching of previous popes on religious liberty. Such development could not have occurred "unless theologians and bishops had been free to be critical of papal teaching, to express views at variance with it." After detailing the conditions for legitimate dissent (competence, sincere effort to assent, convincing contrary reasons), Arzube argues that dissent must be viewed as "something positive and constructive" in the life of the Church.[8]

A similar attitude is clear in a recent pastoral letter of Bishop Michael Pfeifer (San Angelo). When he speaks of official teaching, he states:

> Official teaching cannot replace the responsibility of Catholics to seek the truth in those teachings and to give their assent to that truth. And no one of us can simply sit back and wait for church authorities or theologians to figure things out or to make up our minds for us. This responsibility and freedom is nowhere more evident than in the areas where no final assurance can be given that God's own truth has been found.[9]

In cases like this, the church offers guidance "according to the best available resources at its disposal." But because the teaching is not final, "both church authorities and Catholics in general must be open to ongoing exploration and even revision when greater clarity emerges. This ongoing exploration is carried out especially by theologians."[10]

Thus we see two remarkably different approaches to the magisterium. Behind these attitudes it is easy to discern basic differences in some quite fundamental concepts: (1) revelation: a thoroughly given *depositum*, interpreted propositionally, versus a skeletal one that must be interpreted contextually; (2) the function of theology: the repetition of traditional formulas versus exploration and testing of new formulations; (3) the role of theologians in an academic setting: extension of the magisterium versus personal inquirer; (4) authoritative teaching and the response due to it: obedience versus critical assimilation; (5) the process required in implementing the so-called hierarchical charism of truth; (6) notions or models of the church.

All of those factors, and perhaps many more, play a role in one's concept of the magisterium and its proper functioning. But the key factor is, I believe, the notion of the church. Other differences are largely symptoms of one's model of the church. Diverging models of the church lead to two remarkably different attitudes toward official teaching.

Divergent Models of the Church

An illustration will make this clear. I will use the notion of *sensus fidelium* to highlight this difference. (I use *sensus fidelium* here to refer to the experience and reflection of the faithful. I realize that the concept demands much more precision than I will give it here.)

One view states that this *sensus* ought to be listened to but that it is the ultimate responsibility of authoritative teachers to determine the truth. For example, if large segments of the church believe that the ordination of women is compatible with the gospel and doctrinal development, yet the Congregation for the Doctrine of the Faith (CDF) determines otherwise, then the CDF is right because it is authoritative.

The other view believes that the *sensus* is absolutely essential to a certain and binding proclamation of the truth. Concretely, if large segments of the community do not grasp or accept the arguments and conclusions of an authoritative teacher (e.g., the recent rejection by the CDF of in vitro fertilization between husband and wife), it is a sign that the teaching is not ripe for closure, is badly formulated, or is even inaccurate.

Bishops of the first view see their task as telling people what is right; bishops of the second view tend to see their task as discovering with us the morally right and wrong. Bishops of the first view see the magisterium in terms of certainty and clarity; bishops of the second view are much more likely to hesitate, to question, and to doubt. Bishops of the first view regard dissent (and even openness) as disloyalty; bishops of the second view see dissent as the necessary condition for moral and doctrinal advance and purification. Bishops of the first view see moral and doctrinal truth in terms of authoritative formulations of it; bishops of the second view are more aware of doctrinal development and the changing nature of our concrete personhood. While such sweeping generalizations do not always escape caricature, the abiding substantial point remains valid.

In what follows I want to present two scenarios of the magisterium, two sets of cultural variables that affect the notions of church and of teaching—and therefore of the magisterium, which is the *church teaching*. I shall entitle these the "preconciliar model" and the "postconciliar model." By "preconciliar" I refer to centuries following the Council of Trent and ending with the Second Vatican Council. "Postconciliar" refers to the period from 1962 to the present. I am especially interested in examining dissent against the background of these two scenarios.

The Preconciliar Model

The variables are as follows:

1. The self-definition of the church. For years the juridical model prevailed, the pyramidal model of the manuals with truth and authority descending from above, from Rome. In this model the very term *church* (as in "the church has always taught") referred to a small group in authority in the church.

2. Mass media. For years the information flow in the church and world was slow and restricted. This allowed opinions to be formed without the richness of contribution from varying traditions. Furthermore, authentic formulations were

received less critically and retained a formative influence sometimes disproportionate to their inherent value.

3. Complexity of issues. For many decades Catholic education was defensive. Our seminaries were isolated sanctuaries. These are but symbols of the fact that ecclesial attitudes could take shape without full exposure to contemporary sciences and disciplines and, therefore, at times without an existential awareness of the complexity of issues.

4. Authority. Authority was highly centralized; consultation was quite limited. Oswald von Nell-Breuning composed *Quadragesimo anno* without consultors or critics. The official version of *Casti connubii* was altered in *Acta apostolicae sedis* because the Vatican Latinist misrepresented the mind of Franciscus Hurth on punitive sterilization. After the definition of papal infallibility, it was—and still is—in some circles unthinkable to question papal statements, a development that reached its pinnacle in *Humani generis*, as Congar has noted.

5. Lay and clergy education. For many centuries the clergy were the best-educated persons in the church, not least because they had access to higher education. In such a situation it is understandable that the clergy would assume responsibilities that might be differently dispersed in other areas.

6. Ecclesial groups existed in an atmosphere of polite warfare. Protestants, all Protestants, were the *adversarii* of Catholic doctrinal and moral theses. Their doctrinal and moral writings were forbidden reading. Catholics did not turn to those writings as sources of wisdom. Their very separation from the one true church was a presumption against their orthodoxy.

7. Educational styles. The "master concept" dominated seminary and university teaching, the "hand down" notion of teaching where the professor dictated from his notes, which were often yellow with age. This was rendered viable and possible by uniformity of philosophy and language in the church.

Now, I want to argue that if we take these variables, shake, and mix them, they generated a notion of teaching in the church with the following characteristics. First, there was an undue distinction between teaching and learning, with a rather unique emphasis on the right to teach but with very little being said about the duty to learn first. Second, there was an undue identification of the teaching function with a single group, the hierarchy. Finally, there was an undue isolation of a single function in teaching—the decisive or final word. *Roma locuta causa finita.* For many people the magisterium meant the hierarchical issuance of authoritative decrees.

Catholic theology supported these notions. Catholics laid a heavy stress on the authority of the teacher. The conclusion was as sound as the authority was legitimate. The response to these teachings was heavily obediential. Catholics were to submit and had an obligation to assent. The theologian's task, in the words of Pius XII, was to defend the teaching of the hierarchy.

The Postconciliar Model

The variables changed in the postconciliar scenario.

1. The self-definition of the church. The church now defines itself as the people of God, a *communio*. The model is concentric. The people are the repository of wisdom. As Josef Cardinal Suenens put it, "The pyramid of the old manuals was reversed."[11]

2. Mass media. We live in the age of instancy, of instant communication. Canon Louis Janssens writes an obscure probe in *Ephemerides Theologicae Lovanienses*, and it is reported in *Newsweek* a few weeks later. An even more obscure theologian writes a rather conservative essay on neonatal intensive care in *Journal of the American Medical Association* and is banned in Melbourne a week later. Rapid communica-

tion suggests that the laity is better informed than ever, if not always wiser than ever.

3. Complexity of issues. Catholics are now profoundly immersed in the social and intellectual world about them. They are exposed to many modes of thought. Their seminaries are cheek-by-jowl with the great universities of the country. In sum, they exist in an atmosphere highlighting the genuine complexity of moral and doctrinal issues.

4. Authority. Collegiality prevails, and theoretically, at least, at all levels—papal, episcopal, parochial. The church mimics in its internal life and organization the currents of the secular world in which it lives. It is no accident that collegiality emerged in the church at the very time secular institutions were captivated by democratic processes and shared decision making.

5. Lay and clergy education. Higher education is now widely available; intense specialization is common. Laypersons are often capable of relating their experience and expertise to doctrinal matters in a most enlightening way. Vatican II recognized this when it stated:

> Laymen should also know that it is generally the function of their well-formed Christian conscience to see that the divine law is inscribed in the life of the earthly city. From priests they may look for spiritual light and nourishment. Let the layman not imagine that his pastors are always such experts, that to every problem which arises, however complicated, they can readily give him a concrete solution, or even that such is their mission. Rather, enlightened by Christian wisdom and giving close attention to the teaching authority of the Church, let the layman take on his own distinctive role.[12]

This paragraph is a final farewell to the "dependency syndrome" in Catholic moral and pastoral formation and practice.

6. Ecclesial groups now exist in ecumenical sunshine. Those who were *adversarii* are now separated brothers and sisters. Vatican II recognized this when it stated, "In fidelity

to conscience, Christians are joined with the rest of men in the search for truth and for the genuine solution to the numerous problems which arise in the life of individuals and from social relationships."

7. Educational styles. Catholics now have student involvement, experimentation, and creativity. They have discussion, seminars, cross-disciplinary dialogue. Philosophical uniformity has long disappeared from the scene.

A Wider View of the Magisterium

These remarkable and rather massive sea changes have generated or, perhaps more accurately, should generate a modified notion of teaching in the church, the magisterium. This modified notion has three characteristics. First, the learning process is seen as essential to the teaching process. Second, teaching is a multidimensional function, only one aspect of which is the decisive, the judgmental. Third, teaching therefore involves the charisms of all of us.

Theology itself reflects these changes in its emphases and language. There is more attention to evidence and analysis. As Avery Dulles notes, sound teaching must persuade, not merely command.[13] The proper response is not obedience (we do not obey teachers *qua* teachers). It is rather a docile personal attempt to assimilate—which is my private rendition of *obsequium religiosum* of *Lumen gentium* (no. 25). Others might word the matter more boldly: *Roma locuta, conversatio incepta.* One of my favorite authors is Christopher Butler, former abbot of Downside and auxiliary bishop of London. When dealing with the response due the ordinary magisterium, Butler speaks of a "welcoming gratitude along with the keen alertness of a critical mind and with a good will concerned to play its part both in the purification and the development of the Church's understanding of her inheritance."[14]

I doubt that the matter can be put more accurately or

persuasively. What Butler is more than suggesting is that "the keen alertness of a critical mind" is an essential part of what I like to call the teaching-learning *process* of the church. Without that essential part, the process will be enfeebled, as I believe it has been through short-circuiting of this process.

Butler's phrase reflects Karl Rahner's notion of person as *ein kritisches Wesen*. Rahner says, "All the energies of a living Christianity can be implemented only in a process which must inevitably have a critical component."[15]

It is within this wider understanding of church and magisterium that an assessment of dissent should occur. Concretely, if I dissent, it is the *end* of a process, a docile attempt to assimilate. This process must be prayerful, arduous, reflective. Otherwise there is no *learning*.

My point is that responsible dissent is not just a temporary *end* to a search. It is and must be seen as a new beginning, a beginning of new evidence in the church. If large segments of competent and demonstrably loyal Catholics disagree with certain formulations of *Humanae vitae*, this must be seen as the beginning of a new reflection. Otherwise we have ruled personal reflection out of order in the learning process of the church—and that is intolerable.

In this perspective, the magisterial function in the church is much more a matter of a teaching-learning *process* in which dissent should play a positive, nonthreatening role. It is part of the ordinary way of progress in human growth in understanding. We must learn to institutionalize it and profit from it far more than we have if the moral magisterium is to be an ecumenically viable reality. I say this with considerable confidence rooted in backing from a well-known Continental thinker. He wrote:

> The structure of a human community is correct only if it admits not just the presence of a justified opposition, but also that effectiveness of opposition which is required by the common good and the right of participation.[16]

These words of Karol Wojtyla in *The Acting Person* are no less true of the church than any community.

In summary, then, since Vatican II there has been a move from classical consciousness to historical consciousness. This shift must be allowed to impact on the notion of the moral magisterium if this reality is to operate effectively in our time. The move I refer to has meant a change in outlook on the church as teacher in two ways.

Context

First, the context has changed to include:

1. The loss of what Karl Rahner has called homogeneous culture.

2. The emergence of awareness about the historical relativity of authoritative statements—scriptural, traditional, magisterial.

3. A new awareness that the authoritative tradition is no longer mediated exclusively by the ecclesiastical magisterium but also by autonomous principles, criteria, historical investigation.

4. A collapse of the unitary method and language in theology.

5. The collapse of the theologian as the *uomo universale*.

Specific Points

Second, there is remarkable modification on *specific points:*

1. Criticism of a purely juridical description of theologians and the magisterium, whereby theologians speak only as extensions or delegates of the pope and bishops.

2. A newly recovered conviction about the subordination of the magisterium to scripture and tradition—a kind of

qualification of the idea of magisterium as the *regula fidei proxima*.

3. A new awareness of the inadequacy of "formal" or "official" authority. Authority must vindicate itself.

4. A pervasive conviction that the "assistance of the Spirit" must refer to the whole church.

5. A fresh awareness of the intrinsic need of theological reasoning in communal church discernment.

6. A new sense of the variety of modes in which the magisterium is exercised. There is the realistic sense of the possibility of failure, of inadequacy in official formulations.

In summary, I believe it is accurate to say that we are viewing teaching in the church from the perspective of different cultural variables and a correspondingly altered consciousness. In our time, dissent is viewed as a contribution to a process of growth, not as a challenge to a superior. If the church is conceived in juridical terms within a classical consciousness, dissent is viewed with alarm, as disturbing unity and challenging superiors. The standard phrases to convey this sense are "disturbing the faithful" and "confusion of the faithful." Yet is it not true that when Jesus confronts us we ought to be disturbed? He challenges everything we stand for.

In conclusion, I want to note that in the past five years the American bishops have produced two remarkable pastorals touching on moral questions (one on peace, the other on the economy). The process was open and revisionary. All points of view were welcomed and weighed. This is a very healthy sign. It is a sign of a growing reshaping of the teaching office. That is indispensable. The values of the magisterium will be preserved only if we see it as both a privilege and a responsibility, something we receive but also something to which we contribute. If we are to continue to enjoy the privilege we must incur the responsibility. Our responsibilities are those of docile, loyal, yet critical Catholics who have both the humility and the courage to be led. I say "courage" because in our time to be properly led means to share the burdens of the leader, even if we are hurt in the process, even if we are wrong.

This open, participative process is in marked contrast to the method followed where questions of personal morality (e.g., sexual) are involved. The 1987 document *Instruction on Respect for Human Life in Its Origin and on the Dignity of Procreation* is the latest example. No one has any idea of who the consultants were. Footnotes are exclusively to previous official documents. Ecumenical input was apparently nonexistent; and despite its considerable merits, the document flew in the face of a developing theological consensus that certain procedures such as in vitro fertilization with embryo transfer are morally acceptable under certain conditions.

This consensus is ecumenically significant. Many non-Catholics would welcome a teaching and unifying voice in the moral sphere. However, if the procedures of the magisterium are perceived to violate some basic canons of enquiry, such a magisterium will continue to be a stumbling block to unity rather than its facilitator.

The Effects of Inhibition and Coercion

In the contemporary church Catholics are experiencing an atmosphere of inhibition and coercion. Such an atmosphere can easily have certain impacts:

1. *The weakening of the episcopal magisterium.* Here Catholics should recall the theological force of episcopal agreement described in *Lumen gentium* (no. 25). If the bishops around the world are united with the pope in their teaching, then that teaching can achieve a greater level of stability and certainty and indeed can achieve infallible status if the teaching is a proper object of infallibility and is presented as something to be held definitively. But the unity must be genuine and clear.

In a coercive atmosphere both the genuineness and clarity are put in serious doubt. Here we should recall, regarding genuineness, one of the arguments made during the deliberations of the so-called Birth Control Commission. It was contended that the church could not modify its teaching on birth control regulation because that teaching had been proposed unanimously by the bishops with the pope over a long period of time. To this point Cardinal Suenens replied: "We have heard arguments based on 'what the bishops all taught for decades.' Well, the bishops did defend the classical position. But it was imposed on them by authority. The bishops didn't study the pros and cons. They received directives, they bowed to them, and they tried to explain them to their congregations."[17] In a coercive atmosphere people will repeat things because they are told to and are threatened with punishment if they say anything else. Episcopal unity is revealed as enforced, not genuine.

As for clarity, the more likely scenario in a coercive atmosphere is that the bishops (some at least) will say nothing if they disagree. In such circumstances, to read episcopal silence as unanimity is self-deceptive. Many Catholics have known this, of course. Some years ago I authored with Corrine Bayley, C.S.J., an article proposing that sterilizations in certain instances could be justified.[18] A bishop friend remarked to me: "I can name a hundred bishops who agree with you, but not one who will say so publicly." What seemed unanimity (if only in silence) clearly was not.

When the genuineness and clarity of episcopal agreement have been cast into grave doubt by a coercive atmosphere, the episcopal magisterium itself has been undermined. The meaning of consensus has been eviscerated. The bishops should be the first ones to protest this diminishment of their magisterium and the atmosphere that grounds it.

2. *The weakening of the papal magisterium.* This follows from the first point. If bishops are not speaking their true sentiments, then clearly the pope is not able to draw on the wisdom and reflection of the bishops in the exercise of his ordinary magisterium. When this happens, the presumption

of truth in papal teaching is weakened because such a presumption assumes, as Karl Rahner so repeatedly argued, that the ordinary sources of human understanding have been consulted. That is why what is called the "enforcement of doctrine" is literally counterproductive. It weakens the very vehicle (papal magisterium) that proposes to be the agent of strength and certainty.

3. *The marginalization of theologians*. Coercive measures will almost certainly have the effect of quieting theologians, at least on certain issues. This further erodes both the episcopal and papal magisterium by silencing yet another source of understanding and growth. Archbishop Rembert Weakland has several times underlined this. Many bishops, most recently James Malone, have noted the absolute necessity of theology for their work. In Malone's words, "As a bishop in an episcopal conference which has devoted substantial time and energy to the place of the Church in the world, I can testify to the irreplaceable role of the theological enterprise."[19] If reputable theologians are marginalized, the magisterium is proportionately weakened. And it is no response to exclude from the "reputable" category those with whom one disagrees. That begs the—or any—question.

4. *The demoralization of priests*. When juridical coercion (which is not altogether out of place) too easily dominates the church's teaching-learning process, priests and other ministers become demoralized because they are expected to be the official spokespersons for positions they cannot always and in every detail support. Thus they become torn between their official loyalties and their better judgment and compassion. The journal *Commonweal* has referred to this as "occupational schizophrenia." Archbishop John Quinn adverted to this in the Synod of 1980.[20]

5. *The reduction of the laity*. Coercive insistence on official formulations tells the laity in no uncertain terms that their experience and reflection make little difference in spite of

Vatican II's contrary assertion: "Let it be recognized that all of the faithful—clerical and lay—possess a lawful freedom of enquiry and of thought, and the freedom to express their minds humbly and courageously about those matters in which they enjoy competence."[21] If such humble and courageous expression counts for nothing, we experience yet another wound to the authority of the ordinary magisterium. The search for truth falls victim to ideology.

6. *The compromise of future ministry.* When a rigid orthodoxy is imposed on seminarians in the name of unity and order, the very ability of these future priests to minister to post-Vatican II Catholics is seriously jeopardized. I have seen this happen. Many thousands of Catholics have studied and struggled to assimilate the Council's perspectives. They do not understand and will not accept a new paternalism in moral pedagogy. This means frustration and crisis for the minister trained to practice such a pedagogy.

7. *The loss of the Catholic leaven.* Coercive insistence that the term "official teaching" is simply synonymous with right, certain, sound, and unchangeable (an identification powerfully supported by the suppression of any public dissent) will lead to the public perception that the role of Catholic scholars is an "intellectual form of 'public relations,'" to borrow from Clifford Longley.[22] That means the serious loss of theological credibility in precisely those areas of modern development (e.g., science and technology) where the church should desire to exercise a formative influence. The present pontiff wants both to unite the church and to shape the world, both utterly laudable apostolic objectives. The means to the former could doom the latter.

Christ did not promise us that as individuals we would always be right when deliberating about the practical implications of "being in Christ." He did not promise that the ultimate official teaching would always be right. He did say, *in the fact of our being a community* of believers, that there is no

better way of walking a narrow path than to walk it together—
with the combined eyes and strength and experience of the
entire people, all supporting each other's charisms and gifts.

Notes

1. Charles E. Curran, *Origins* 16 (1986): 181–82.
2. Joseph Cardinal Ratzinger, *Origins* 16 (1986): 203.
3. *National Catholic News Service* news release.
4. This phraseology was recently repeated by John Paul II in a speech to a group of natural family planning experts. He stated, "What is taught by the Church on contraception does not belong to material freely debatable among theologians." *Catholic Messenger*, Davenport, Iowa, 11 June 1987.
5. Yves Congar, O.P., "A Brief History of the Forms of the Magisterium and Its Relations with Scholars," in Charles E. Curran and Richard A. McCormick, S.J., eds., *Readings in Moral Theology*, no. 3 (Paramus, N.J.: Paulist/Newman Press, 1982), 325.
6. Joseph Farraher, S.J., "Why Don't Bishops Take Action Against Dissenters?" *Homiletic and Pastoral Review* 79, no. 7 (April 1979): 64–66.
7. Kenneth Baker, S.J., "Magisterium and Theologians," *Homiletic and Pastoral Review* 79, no. 7 (April 1979): 14–23.
8. Juan Arzube, "When Is Dissent Legitimate?" *Catholic Journalist* (June 1978): 9.
9. Michael Pfeifer, O.M.I., "Thoughts on Freedom, Conscience and Obedience," *Origins* 16 (1986): 391–92.
10. Ibid.
11. *National Catholic Reporter*, 28 May 1969.
12. *Documents of Vatican II*, ed. Walter M. Abbott, S.J. (New York: America Press, 1966), 244.
13. Avery Dulles, S.J., "The Two Magisteria: an Interim Reflection," *Proceedings of the Catholic Theological Society of America* 35 (1980): 155–69.
14. B. Christopher Butler, "Authority and the Christian Conscience," *Clergy Review* 60 (1975): 3–17.

15. Karl Rahner, *Theological Investigations* (New York: Crossroad, 1981), 17:135, footnote.
16. Karol Wojtyla, *The Acting Person* (Boston and Dordrecht, Neth.: D. Reidel Publishing Co., 1979), 286–87.
17. Robert Blair Kaiser, *The Politics of Sex and Religion* (Kansas City: Leaven, 1985), 170.
18. Corrine Bayley, C.S.J., and Richard A. McCormick, S.J., "Sterilization: The Dilemma of Catholic Hospitals," *America* 143 (1980): 222–25.
19. James Malone, "How Bishops and Theologians Relate," *Origins* 16 (1986): 169–74.
20. John R. Quinn, "New Context for Contraception Teaching," *Origins* 10 (1980): 263–67.
21. "The Church in the Modern World," no. 62, in *Documents of Vatican II*, ed. Walter M. Abbott, S.J. (New York: America Press, 1966), 270.
22. Clifford Longley, "Cynicism and Sexual Morality," *Times*, London, 4 August 1986.

CHAPTER 6

Religious Teaching in Secular Form

James M. Wall

DURING THE SPRING OF EACH YEAR, THE ATTENTION OF many of us tends to focus upon graduating classes. The school year ends, and in various ways we are expected to provide words of advice to graduates. Faced with this assignment recently, I looked to one of my favorite sources, the movies. Casting back in my memory I wondered just what was the best-known piece of advice I had ever heard on screen. Not surprisingly, I thought of a line from one of my favorite movies, released over twenty years ago. Most of you will recall it, and you may have even seen it recently on cable or videocassette.

The film's title, appropriately enough, is *The Graduate*, starring a much younger Dustin Hoffman as a college graduate who returns to his California home to decide how to spend the rest of his life. You may remember that the film opens with that marvelous Simon and Garfunkle song "Sounds of Silence" as Benjamin Braddock leaves the plane and walks down the Los Angeles Airport concourse.

126

The lyrics of the song begin, "Hello darkness, my old friend, I've come to talk with you again," not exactly a rousing note of approval for the home toward which Benjamin is traveling. That evening, at a party given by his parents, Benjamin is pulled aside by an older man, a friend of his father, who speaks to him with all the solemnity the older generation can muster when imparting wisdom to the young.

The older man tells Benjamin he has just one word to say to him. Benjamin assures him that he is listening for that one word. After a pause, the older man intones, gravely, "Plastics." Puzzled, Benjamin wonders if maybe there is more to be said, but there is nothing more to be added; there is a great future in plastics.

Immediately after that scene Benjamin retreats upstairs to his room and stares into the goldfish tank, contemplating, perhaps, his future in plastics.

That was twenty years ago. Today the word might be "microchips," for what is being conveyed here is a guiding worldview with which Benjamin Braddock, the graduate, should greet his future. It is a worldview that David Tracy, in the *Analogical Imagination*,[1] indicates is governed by a techno-economic value system, that set of priorities which revolve around the bottom line. The one word given to Benjamin is "plastics," indicating that for the rest of his life he should gear his existence around the motif of success and financial gain. His security is to be found in the things of this world.

Benjamin is hearing the final word in a story, the climax of which is that his future will mean nothing unless it involves the most successful business career he can pursue. It is the story of a society rooted in a techno-economic value system.

Surely there is a different story which the Christian community has to offer Benjamin and his sons and daughters twenty years later. There is. And we turn for the source to a collection of writings novelist Reynolds Price describes as "a fixed and clearly legible story, unprecedented in the known history of earlier religions and never successfully imitated."

Price, in his essay "The Origins and Life of Narrative," refers to

> the canonical sacred tales of Jews and Christians. Those tales
> . . . are their own best witness to the ancient conviction of a
> sizable portion of the human race that a handful of [persons]
> over two thousands years ago on a piece of land larger than the
> state of North Carolina were brought into intermittent contact
> with an inhuman power quite beyond that available to com-
> parable tales from other witnesses without our tradition—
> Assyria, Egypt, Greece.[2]

An Openness to Mystery

Given the power of that description of the scriptures which form the base for our religious community, it would seem reasonable to presume that the way to confront the inadequacy of the "plastics" worldview would be to repeat the canonical sacred tales and wait for their power to begin to work on the listener. But in today's secular society this is not as easy to accomplish as it might have been during the period when the sacred tales were first put into narrative form.

Why is this so? Price traces the development of what he describes as "the only perfect story"—these sacred tales—as coming into existence because of the voracious hunger of our historical parents "for origins and causes, operating upon the always ready mass of mystery, and the even more basic hunger for solace. . . ."[3]

The need for solace continues, and the voracious hunger is unabated. But what is missing in secular society is a receptivity to the "always ready mass of mystery," for an openness to mystery has been replaced by a techno-economic worldview in which the highest values are rooted in success, not mystery. One of Benjamin Braddock's spiritual sons shows up in a recent movie directed by Oliver Stone, *Wall Street*, in which the Faustian legend is reenacted. A young stockbroker, eager for financial success and power, readily agrees with an older man to follow his directions in much the way Faust listened to Mephisto. There would be no time for pausing to contemplate the mysteries of life; all attention would be focused on financial success.

In order, then, to be receptive to that "perfect story" that has been related to us in the canonical tales, we must be open to the mystery of the One who lives this story within history, announcing to humankind that the bottom line is not plastics but love. But this announcement cannot be heard unless we have the capacity to receive mystery.

What is this term *mystery?* The novelist Flannery O'Connor says, "The fiction writer presents mystery through manners, grace through nature, but when (s)he finishes, there always has to be left over that sense of Mystery which cannot be accounted for by any human formula."[4] We turn to O'Connor for a definition of mystery, for like so many of those creative persons who employ fiction to probe for the depths of existence, she recognized that at the heart of human existence lies the potential for an encounter with that which is greater than the sum of all the profits we can make in many lifetimes.

We need plastics, and we need microchips to function within our secular world; but without a sensitivity and openness to the mystery we encounter at the heart of existence, we are left with a meaningless worldview. Contrast this sense of meaninglessness, which reflects a plastics worldview, with a portion of the New Testament passage in which a woman of Samaria asks how it is possible that a Jew would request a drink of water from a non-Jew, a Samaritan. Jesus, who had made the initial request for a drink, answers, "If you knew who it is that is saying to you, 'Give me a drink,' you would have asked him and he would have given you living water." What sort of language is this? Living water? It is the language of mystery.

And mystery is not some puzzle that is waiting to be solved; nor is it a plot moving toward complete resolution. No, Ulti-

mate Mystery is the incarnation of that which is more than the
reality we can perceive in secular form. It is that dimension
which addresses us in the depths of personal despair or in the
heights of joy.

So why the inability to receive this living water? The
woman from Samaria is the quintessential modern person
who, practical-minded, thinks in terms of rational thought in
order to make sense of daily events. Like her, when con-
fronted with the incarnational mystery, we each echo her
answer when presented with the gift of living water, "Sir, you
have nothing to draw with, and the well is deep."

In our natural state, as Paul might have put it, we resist the
notion of mystery by demanding facticity in our encounters.
In *The Sportswriter*, novelist Richard Ford tells the story of
Frank Bascombe, a divorced man whose two children now live
with his estranged wife. One Easter Sunday morning he
wakes and thinks of his children:

> [She] I know, is not taking Paul and Clarissa to church, a fact
> which worries me—not because they will turn out godless (I
> couldn't care less) but because she is bringing them up to be
> perfect little factualists and information accumulators with no
> particular reverence or speculative interest for what's not
> known.[5]

Stories or narratives do not generate mystery. They do not
argue for or against mystery. What they do is offer us the
possibility of encountering mystery. And in what Reynolds
Price sums up as "the perfect story"—the narrative which
begins with the classic phrase "in the beginning" and pro-
ceeds to a moment when mystery is manifest in the death and
resurrection of the Christ—we have our revelation of mystery.

It awaits our acceptance. But it is our burden, shared with
the woman from Samaria, that we resist the gift of mystery
when it comes to us in the "perfect story" or when it comes to
us in creative, imaginative form in secular renderings. Novels,
plays, films do not need to reproduce "the greatest story ever

told" to offer us this mystery. What these imaginative forms do is replicate through a variety of stories the deepest mystery of a God who creates, sustains, and—wonder of all wonders—actually cares.

The director Fred Zinnemann recalls the decision to cast Montgomery Clift as Private Prewitt in the film based on the James Jones novel *From Here to Eternity*. If you recall the story, Prewitt was, in Jones's description, a "deceptively slim young man" who was forced into a boxing match which he could not win. Zinnemann continues, "1 wanted Clift because the story was not about a fellow who didn't want to box; it was a story about the human spirit refusing to be broken, about a man who resists all sorts of pressure from an institution he loves, who becomes an outsider and eventually dies for it."[6]

That summary of the role Prewitt plays in *From Here to Eternity* is not an exact parallel to another story of a man who was misunderstood and finally crucified; but there are similarities, not because either Jones or Zinnemann wanted to replicate the gospel story in their stories, but because the gospel story is the central story which stands as the revelation of both the human situation and of the God who redeems that situation.

We do not ask our imaginative forms to serve us homiletically; we only ask them to probe for us the depths of mystery. If we have allowed the central story of the revelation of that mystery to penetrate our lives, then we are ready to receive further intimations of that same revelation in secular forms. An openness to story is essential to our humanness. As Reynolds Price says in his discussion of narrative:

> The root of story sprang from need—need for companionship and consolation by a creature as vulnerable, four million years ago and now, as any protozoan in a warm brown swamp. The need is not for the total consolation of narcotic fantasy—our own will performed in airless triumph—but for credible news that our lives proceed in order toward a pattern which, if tragic here and now, is ultimately pleasing in the mind of a God who

sees a totality and *at last* enacts his will. We crave nothing less than perfect story; and while we chatter or listen all our lives in a din or craving—jokes, anecdotes, novels, dreams, films, plays, songs, half the words of our days—we are satisfied only by the one short tale we feel to be true: History is the story of the will of a just God who knows us.[7]

Intimations of Mystery

At the heart of the ultimate story the mystery of God awaits us. Meanwhile we find intimations of its awesome message in the creative forms produced by others who probe for that mystery without necessarily naming it in the same terms.

In Tom Stoppard's play *Jumpers*, George, a professor of philosophy, is talking with his friend Dotty. They are arguing over the church and God. Dotty speaks, "Archie says the church is a monument to irrationality. . . ."

George turns and shouts at her with surprising anger:

The National Gallery is a monument to irrationality! Every concert hall is a monument to irrationality—and so is a nicely kept garden, or a lover's favor, or a home for stray dogs! If rationality were the criterion for things being allowed to exist, the world would be one gigantic field of soya beans![8]

Marshall Berman, in his provocative book *All that Is Solid Melts into Air,*[9] describes Goethe's Faust as the quintessential modern person, the individual who believes in the inevitability of progress and in his ability to produce that progress. Faust is driven to conquer all he confronts, because in his special deal with Mephisto, the devil, he has agreed that the world is his to control so long as he does not ever again pause and say to any part of the world, "du bist so schön," "You are so beautiful."

For the promise of power, control, and all that he wants, Faust must yield only one thing—his freedom to love the world he is conquering. It seems like a good bargain at first, since in his modernity he assumes that love may be bought and that the mystery that reveals the true nature of love is but a superstition that went out of style with the coming of scientific wisdom.

Through the telling of this classic tale, Goethe invites us to break the bonds of modernity and accept the gift of the One who addresses us through Mystery. In his bargain with the devil, Faust is not led to do evil; on the contrary, he uses his power to do good. He employs modern techniques to banish NEED, WANT, GUILT, and CARE; and, though he does manage to banish this quartet of plagues, to his dismay he finds that though he eliminates them from the outer world under his control, they all return to his inner world; and though he shoves them aside, CARE remains and breathes on him, striking him blind.

As Goethe records this moment, CARE "touches him, and she tells him that he has been blind all along; it is out of inner darkness that all his visions and all his actions have grown."[10] Faust has been racing through life, using his powers to solve problems; but in his compact with Mephisto he has given up his freedom to see the world and exclaim *"du bist so schön."* He has remained blind to the deeper realities of life; he has missed the ultimate Mystery.

In speaking of his film *2001: A Space Odyssey*, director Stanley Kubrick says he agrees with Arthur C. Clarke, the author of the original story on which the film is based, when he wrote, "Sometimes I think we are alone in the universe and sometimes I think we aren't; in both cases the idea makes me dizzy."[11] And indeed, it would. The remedy for this dizziness is a story told through a biblical narrative and repeated in a variety of forms whenever imaginative authors probe the mystery to find that "history is the story of the will of a just God who knows us."

A pastor's assignment then, should he or she wish to accept it, is to offer that word in place of plastics or microchips. It is a word that is supplemented and reinforced in secular form because the just God who knows us has never confined revelation to predictable forms. All around us are burning bushes. We need only to recognize their presence and stand before them in awe.

Notes

1. David Tracy, *Analogical Imagination* (New York: Crossroad, 1986).
2. Reynolds Price, "The Origins and Life of Narrative" in *A Palpable God* (Berkeley: North Point Press, 1985), 29.
3. Ibid., 28.
4. Sally and Robert Fitzgerald, *Flannery O'Connor: Mystery and Manners, Occasional Prose* (New York: Farrar, Straus & Cudahy, 1961), 153.
5. Richard Ford, *The Sportswriter* (New York: Random House, 1986), 204.
6. Fred Zinnemann, "From Here to Eternity," *Sight and Sound* (Winter 1987): 21.
7. Price, *A Palpable God*, 14.
8. Tom Stoppard, *Jumpers* (New York: Grove Press, 1974).
9. Marshall Berman, *All that Is Solid Melts into Air* (New York: Simon & Schuster, 1982).
10. Ibid., 71.
11. Michael Ciment, *Kubrick* (New York: Holt, Rinehart & Winston, 1983), 128.